Iglulualumiut Prehistory:
The lost Inuit of Franklin Bay

David Morrison

Archaeological Survey of Canada
Mercury Series Paper 142

Canadian Museum of Civilization

© Canadian Museum of Civilization 1990

Canadian Cataloguing in Publication Data

Morrison, David A.

Iglulualumiut prehistory:
the lost inuit of Franklin Bay, NWT

(Mercury Series, ISSN 0316-1854)
(Paper / Archaeological Survey of Canada,
ISSN 0317-2244 ; no. 142)
Includes abstract in French.
Bibliography: p.
ISBN 0-660-10794-5

1. Franklin Bay (N.W.T.) – Antiquities. 2. Inuit – Northwest Territories – Franklin Bay – Antiquities. 3. Thule culture – Northwest Territories – Franklin Bay. 4. Excavation (Archaeology) – Northwest Territories – Franklin Bay. I. Canadian Museum of Civilization. II. Archaeological Survey of Canada. III. Title. IV. Title: The lost inuit of Franklin Bay. V. Series. VI. Series: Paper (Archaeological Survey of Canada) ; no. 142.

E78.M16 M67 1989   971.9'2   C89-097092-0

Printed and bound in Canada

Published by the
Canadian Museum of Civilization
100 Laurier Street
P.O. Box 3100, Station B
Hull, Quebec
J8X 4H2

Archaeological Survey of Canada
Papers Coordinator:
Richard E. Morlan

Canada

OBJECT OF THE MERCURY SERIES

The Mercury Series is designed to permit the rapid dissemination of information pertaining to the disciplines in which the Canadian Museum of Civilization is active. Considered an important reference by the scientific community, the Mercury Series comprises over three hundred specialized publications on Canada's history and prehistory.

Because of its specialized audience, the series consists largely of monographs published in the language of the author.

In the interest of making information available quickly, normal production procedures have been abbreviated. As a result, grammatical and typographical errors may occur. Your indulgence is requested

Titles in the Mercury Series can be obtained by writing to:

Mail Order Services
Publishing Division
Canadian Museum of Civilization
100 Laurier Street
P.O. Box 3100, Station B
Hull, Quebec
J8X 4H2

BUT DE LA COLLECTION MERCURE

La collection Mercure vise à diffuser rapidement le résultat de travaux dans les disciplines qui relèvent des sphères d'activités du Musée canadien des civilisations. Considérée comme un apport important dans la communauté scientifique, la collection Mercure présente plus de trois cents publications spécialisées portant sur l'héritage canadien préhistorique et historique.

Comme la collection s'adresse à un public spécialisé celle-ci est constituée essentiellement de monographies publiées dans la langue des auteurs.

Pour assurer la prompte distribution des exemplaires imprimés, les étapes de l'édition ont été abrégées. En conséquence, certaines coquilles ou fautes de grammaire peuvent subsister : c'est pourquoi nous réclamons votre indulgence.

Vous pouvez vous procurer la liste des titres parus dans la collection Mercure en écrivant au :

Service des commandes postales
Division de l'édition
Musée canadien des civilisations
100, rue Laurier
C.P. 3100, succursale B
Hull (Québec)
J8X 4H2

Abstract

Very little archaeological work has been accomplished along the southern coast of Amundsen Gulf in the area between the historic ranges of the Mackenzie and Copper Inuit. This monograph compares material from four sites in the Franklin Bay area in the western part of Amundsen Gulf. One is the Iglulualuit site (NlRu-1) near the mouth of the Horton River, excavated by the author in 1987. Two others are sites investigated by the explorer Stefansson in 1911, and the fourth was excavated by John Hadley of the Canadian Arctic Expedition in 1917. Together these four sites represent perhaps 400 years of Inuit cultural development from late Thule times to just prior to European exploration (ca A.D. 1350-1750). Artifact comparisons between Franklin Bay sites and sites from other areas suggest a number of conclusions about the nature of prehistoric Inuit occupations in Amundsen Gulf.

1. A developed form of Thule culture known as the Clachan phase is represented by house sites all along the southern coast of Amundsen Gulf, and into Coronation Gulf. It is stylistically more similar to Alaskan Thule than to analogues in the eastern Canadian Arctic.

2. There is some indication that most of Amundsen Gulf was depopulated by about A.D. 1400 for reasons which remain unknown. A stylistic shift from open to closed socket harpoon heads at about this same time marks the end of the Thule period. Thereafter, there is evidence of human occupation only in the westernmost part of Amundsen Gulf in Franklin Bay.

3. The post-Thule Recent occupation in Franklin Bay is of direct local Thule culture origin, and is stylistically and culturally very similar to the late prehistoric Mackenzie Inuit. In fact, the Franklin Bay people, who can be termed "Iglulualumiut," are probably best considered as a sixth Mackenzie Inuit society and the most easterly of the Western Eskimo.

4. According to historic information, Iglulualumiut society disappeared early in the 19th century due, primarily, to a disease epidemic. Survivors emigrated mainly to Baillie Island at Cape Bathurst.

Résumé

La côte méridionale du golfe Amundsen, entre les aires historiques des Inuit du Mackenzie et des Inuit du cuivre, a rarement fait l'objet de recherches archéologiques. La présente monographie compare des objets recueillis dans quatre sites de la région de la baie Franklin, dans le secteur ouest du golfe Amundsen. Le premier est le site Iglulualuit (NlRu-1), à proximité de l'embouchure de la rivière Horton qui a été fouillé par l'auteur en 1987. Deux autres sites ont été examinés par l'explorateur Stefansson en 1911 tandis que le quatrième a été fouillé par John Hadley, membre de l'Expédition de 1917 dans l'Arctique canadien. En tout, ces quatre sites représentent peut-être 400 ans d'évolution culturelle inuit, depuis le Thulé postérieur jusqu'à la veille de la période d'exploration européenne (soit environ de 1350 à 1750 de notre ère). La comparaison d'objets des divers sites de la baie Franklin et de ceux d'autres régions suggère un certain nombre de conclusions quant à la nature des occupations inuit du golfe Amundsen.

1. Une forme évoluée de la culture Thulé, appelée phase Clachan, est représentée par des emplacements de maisons tout le long de la côte sud du golfe Amundsen, jusque dans la baie du Couronnement. Du point de vue stylistique, elle s'apparente plus à la culture Thulé d'Alaska qu'aux cultures analogues de l'est de l'Arctique canadien.

2. Certains indices permettent de croire que la région du golfe Amundsen s'est presque entièrement dépeuplée vers 1400 ap. J.-C., pour des raisons encore inconnues. A peu près à cette époque, un changement stylistique des têtes de harpon, dont la douille ouverte a été remplacée par une douille fermée, marque la fin de la période Thulé. Par la suite, on trouve des traces d'occupation humaine seulement dans la partie la plus occidentale du golfe Amundsen, dans la baie Franklin.

3.   L'occupation récente de la baie Franklin, post-Thulé, descend directement de la culture Thulé locale et, des points de vue stylistique et culturel, elle ressemble beaucoup à celle de l'époque préhistorique récente des Inuit du Mackenzie. De fait, les habitants de la baie Franklin, qu'on peut appeler "Iglulualumiut", constituent sans doute une sixième société du groupe des Inuit du Mackenzie. Parmi les Esquimaux de l'Ouest, ce sont ceux qui vivent le plus à l'Est.

4.   Selon les sources historiques, la société iglulualumiut a disparu au début du XlX^e siècle, surtout à cause d'une épidémie. Les survivants ont émigré principalement à l'île Baillie, dans la région du cap Bathurst.

Acknowledgements

My thanks go to a great many people and institutions who assisted in the production of this study. Robert McGhee (Archaeological Survey of Canada, Canadian Museum of Civilization) first told me of the Iglulualuit site, and supported my plans to work there. Ray LeBlanc, then of the Archaeological Survey of Canada's Northern Oil and Gas Action Plan, also provided information on local conditions, and assisted with helicopter logistic support. I was ably assisted by my competent field crew: Ken Swayze, Ann O'Sullivan, and Stephen Sellinger. Funds for the Iglulualuit field work were provided by the Northern Oil and Gas Action Plan (NOGAP) and the Archaeological Survey of Canada, Canadian Museum of Civilization. Accommodations in Inuvik were provided by John Osterick and the Inuvik Scientific Resource Centre, while radio contact was supplied by the Polar Continental Shelf Project in Tuktoyaktuk. Thanks go to the community of Paulatuk and the Inuvialuit Land Administration for permission to excavate.

The American Museum of Natural History generously loaned the Stefansson collections from Okat and Langton Bay. Ellen Foulkes did the Iglulualuit cataloguing and assisted in the identification of the bird bones. Darlene Balkwell of the Zooarchaeological Identification Centre (National Museum of Natural Sciences) provided facilities for faunal identification. Graphs and maps are the product David Laverie and wordprocessing was done by Jean-Pierre Allaire.

TABLE OF CONTENTS

Chapter One: **Introduction**..............................pg. 1

Chapter Two: **The Sites**
    Iglulualuit...pg. 8
    Langton Bay...pg. 21
    Okat..pg. 24
    Booth Island..pg. 28

Chapter Three: **Sea Mammal Hunting Gear**
    Iglulualuit...pg. 32
    Langton Bay...pg. 34
    Okat..pg. 37
    Booth Island..pg. 39
    Discussion..pg. 42

Chapter Four: **Land Hunting Gear**
    Iglulualuit...pg. 48
    Langton Bay...pg. 50
    Okat..pg. 52
    Booth Island..pg. 52
    Discussion..pg. 53

Chapter Five: **Fishing Gear**
    Iglulualuit...pg. 57
    Langton Bay...pg. 58
    Okat..pg. 60
    Booth Island..pg. 61
    Discussion..pg. 62

Chapter Six: **Transportation Gear**
    Iglulualuit..pg. 66
    Langton Bay...pg. 66
    Okat..pg. 67
    Booth Island..pg. 67
    Discussion..pg. 68

Chapter Seven: **Men's Tools**
    Iglulualuit..pg. 70
    Langton Bay...pg. 73
    Okat..pg. 74
    Booth Island..pg. 77
    Discussion..pg. 79

Chapter Eight: **Women's Tools and Domestic Items**
    Iglulualuit..pg. 83
    Langton Bay...pg. 88
    Okat..pg. 89
    Booth Island..pg. 91
    Discussion..pg. 94

Chapter Nine: **Chronology and Cultural Position**
    The Thule Period....................................pg. 98
    The Recent Period in Franklin Bay...................pg. 106

Chapter Ten: **Iglulualumiut Prehistory**
    Iglulualumiut Origins...............................pg. 111
    The De-Population of Amundsen Gulf..................pg. 115

References Cited..pg. 120

Plates..pg. 129

CHAPTER 1

INTRODUCTION

At the time of European exploration in the early 19th century, the Inuit[1] living around the mouth of the Mackenzie River were the richest and most culturally sophisticated in Arctic Canada. Numbering about 2500 people organized into at least five territorial groups spread from the Alaska border to Cape Bathurst, they were culturally allied with the Inupiat of north Alaska, much more than with other Canadian Inuit (McGhee 1974; Morrison 1988a). In McGhee's (1988) terms, they were "rich," while other Canadian Inuit were "poor." Their Copper Inuit neighbours to the east, for instance, they considered "outright savages" (Petitot 1970: 215), lacking such amenities as permanent log houses, civic structures (_karigis_), and a stratified social organization. The ecological basis of this disparity is clear from a comparison of population densities, which averaged about one person per twenty-five square-kilometers for the Mackenzie Inuit, and less than one person per 250 square-kilometers in the case of the Copper Inuit. Within the broad territorial divisions of Eskimo culture, the Mackenzie Inuit were the easternmost representatives of the Western Eskimo, while the Copper Inuit were the most westerly of the Central Eskimo.

Dividing these two groups was one of the largest expanses of unoccupied territory in the Canadian Arctic. The first European to visit the area, John Richardson, sailed from the mouth of the Mackenzie River to Coronation Gulf in 1826 (Franklin 1971). He noted villages along the northern coast of the Tuktoyaktuk Peninsula and at Cape Bathurst, but the "last Esquimaux seen" is recorded on the eastern coast of the Cape Bathurst peninsula (Franklin 1971: end map). At Cape Lyon he recorded "some old

---

[1] The Eskimo of Canada and Greenland prefer to be called by their own term "Inuit" ("men", or "people"), while those of northwestern Alaska prefer "Inupiat." The more general term "Eskimo" is retained to refer to both, and to their prehistoric cultural and biological ancestors.

IGLULUALUMIUT PREHISTORY

winter houses" but writes also that "we perceived no indications of the Esquimaux having recently visited this quarter" (in Franklin 1971: 241). Except for the discovery of recent footprints near the mouth of the Croker River (Ibid.: 246), he cites no evidence of Inuit occupation or use along the whole south Amundsen Gulf coast as far as Dolphin and Union Strait. His observations during a second voyage twenty years later present a similar picture (Richardson 1851), as do those of the various other Royal Navy expeditions of the mid-19th century (Pullen 1979, Armstrong 1857, Miertsching 1967, M'Clure 1969). There is a modern Inuit village at Paulatuk, but it is the result of recent immigration (Mackay 1958: 116-119).

The southern coast of Amundsen Gulf is nonetheless an area of considerable importance to anyone attempting to understand the development of Inuit culture in Canada. It is one of only two possible routes along which Thule culture spread into Arctic Canada from Alaska a thousand years ago (the other route being through the Arctic islands). As an event, or series of events, which brought the biological and cultural ancestors of the Canadian Inuit into Arctic Canada, the importance of this migration to Arctic prehistory is difficult to overestimate, yet it remains known in only the crudest outline. And, as we have seen, at a much later date, Amundsen Gulf formed the population hiatus or buffer separating historic Western and Central Eskimo.

Despite its potential importance, the archaeology of Amundsen Gulf has remained essentially unexplored. In 1911, Vihljalmur Stefansson noted a number of archaeological sites in the area, and did some brief excavations at several of them (Stefansson 1913, 1914a). Except for a short note by Wissler (1916), this material has not yet been described. Excavations have also been made by other early 20th-century travellers, such as the Rev. H. Girling (ASC Old Catalogue) and members of the Canadian Arctic Expedition (ASC Old Catalogue). Again none of

CHAPTER 1: INTRODUCTION

FIGURE 1

MACKENZIE AND COPPER INUIT TERRITORIAL RANGES

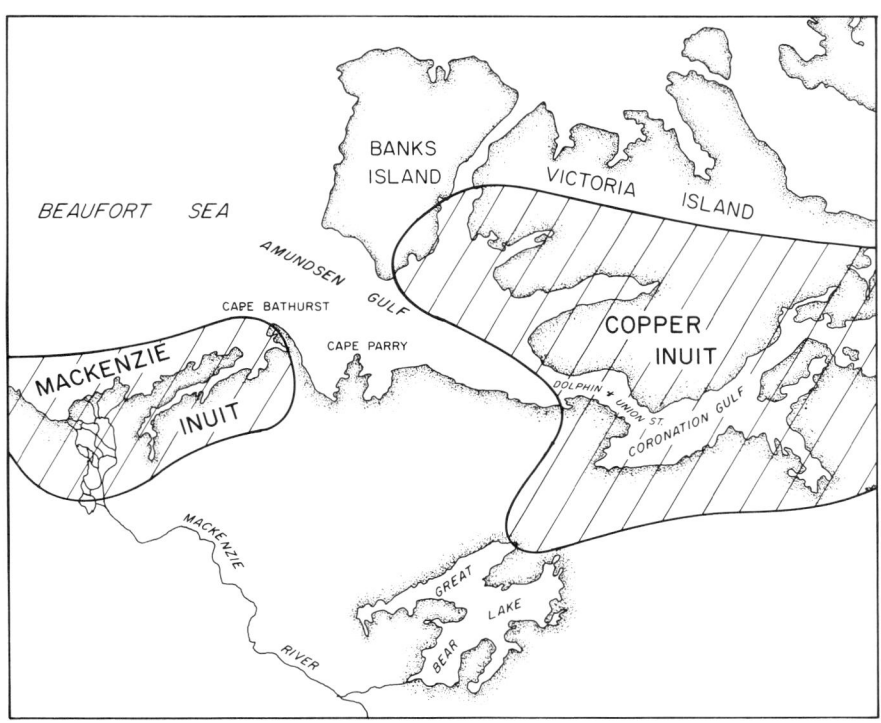

this material has seen more than passing mention in published or manuscript sources. In 1963, William E. Taylor accomplished the only previous work in the area by a trained archaeologist, surveying DEW-line sites between Cape Parry and Cambridge Bay (Taylor 1972). He recorded three sites in the study area, all

IGLULUALUMIUT PREHISTORY

attributable to Thule culture. Two are located at Cape Parry (Jackson and Vaughan) and one further east, at Tysoe Point (Morris). Taylor, with two assistants, was able to spend a total of less than one week at these three sites.

A dearth of archaeological data has been no impediment to hypotheses and suggestions about the nature of Inuit occupations in the area. Stefansson (1914a: 11-12, 17, 25), in particular, felt that the apparently unoccupied nature of Amundsen Gulf during the early historic period was due to the fact that Richardson and other Royal Navy observers sailed too far from shore for trustworthy observation. As late as the middle 19th century, he suggests, there was a continuous string of habitations from Cape Bathurst to Coronation Gulf. From the semi-subterranean house ruins they left behind, he suggested a Mackenzie Inuit-like cultural affiliation, distinguishing them strongly from the Copper Inuit further east, who lived only in tents or snow houses.

Stefansson's suggestion has not been generally accepted, and it is clear that it is based in part on a confusion between ancient Thule house ruins and those of his hypothetical recent occupation (see McGhee 1974: 18). However, the observation of house ruins was not his only source of information. According to Stefansson, the inhabitants of Baillie Island, the most easterly Mackenzie Inuit settlement by the full historic period, believed that people like themselves had lived until very recently in Franklin Bay. A number of villages are mentioned, including Iglulualuit at the mouth of the Horton River, where people from Franklin Bay congregated in the spring to net ringed seals (Ibid.: 352). Other villages were located at Langton Bay and near Point Stivens (Okat), and people also apparently lived around Cape Parry. That they were not members of the Avvaqmiut or Baillie Island territorial group seems clear from the assertion that they rarely travelled as far west as Baillie Island, and then only to trade (Ibid.: 308).

CHAPTER 1: INTRODUCTION

An old woman born at Langton Bay was apparently still living at Baillie Island in the early 20th century. Her name was Panigyuk, and she was estimated to be about 75 years old in 1911 (Ibid.: 307-308). Stefansson never talked directly with her, but through an intermediary learned many topographic details and something of the subsistence economy of the Franklin Bay people. He was also told that Franklin Bay had been abandoned due to starvation, followed by an epidemic. These two events both occurred between the birth and marriage of Panigyuk. She and most of the survivors moved to Baillie Island, probably by about 1845, since she saw Richardson on his second visit there in 1848 (Ibid.: 332; see Richardson 1851: 266-268). Stefansson also repeats the story of a man born at "Langley Bay" (Langton Bay?) who at the age of 12 or 14 moved to Kittigazuit at the mouth of the Mackenzie. As a grown man he returned home to find the area abandoned, although he did find a stone lamp east of Cape Parry which had belonged to his father (Ibid.: 183-184).

Stefansson's model of Amundsen Gulf prehistory thus rests upon two legs. One is his suggestion of a continuous line of settlements over the entire southern coast of Amundsen Gulf, which appears to be based entirely on the observation of house ruins. The second concerns what appears to be an extinct branch of the Mackenzie Inuit living in Franklin Bay, and is based upon the memory of the Baillie Islanders, and the testimony of Panigyuk. Stefansson is fairly scrupulous in distinguishing the two, although he does imply without apparent justification that the Baillie Islanders were aware of people living east of Franklin Bay.

> East of Cape Bathurst there was also a continuous line of settlements as far as Langton Bay probably up to 1840 and a little after. It is true that from an

IGLULUALUMIUT PREHISTORY

> archaeological point of view, it seems fairly clear that the coast for more than one hundred miles further east still, was occupied by people of a cultural affinity with the Mackenzie group; but the feeling of the Baillie Islanders themselves is, that the people further east than Langton Bay were not of their kind (Stefansson 1914a: 11-12).
>
> There is little doubt that there was a continuous chain of habitations prior to say 1830, all the way east along the coast from Langton Bay to Coronation Gulf, and from the character of the archaeological remains, we are inclined to think that these people resembled in culture those of the Baillie Islands more than they did those of Coronation Gulf. However, there seems to have been a feeling at the Baillie Islands that the people east of Langton Bay were not their people, while those of Langton Bay were, and when the changing trade conditions and other reasons broke the continuity of habitation along the coast (about 1840), most of the people of Langton Bay moved west to the Baillie Islands, while some of Langton Bay and apparently all east of them, moved east toward Coronation Gulf if indeed they were not exterminated by some famine...
> (Stefansson 1914a: 25).

The present study examines the archaeology and prehistory of Stefansson's Franklin Bay Inuit. Collections from four sites

CHAPTER 1: INTRODUCTION

FIGURE 2

FRANKLIN BAY AND AMUNDSEN GULF

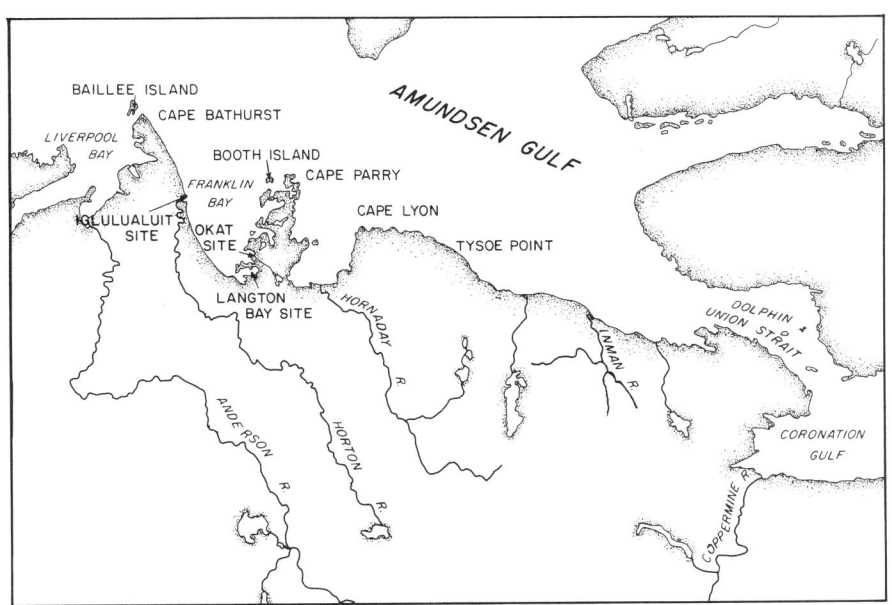

are examined. Three of these relate directly to Stefansson's observations, including Iglulualuit, excavated by the author in 1987, and Okat and Langton Bay, excavated by Stefansson himself in 1911. Also considered is material from a Thule culture site on Booth Island, excavated in 1917 by John Hadley of the Canadian Arctic Expedition. Together, a consideration of these sites allows a cultural definition of the late prehistoric/early historic inhabitants of Franklin Bay, and gives some idea of their prehistoric origins.

Chapter 2
THE SITES
Iglulualuit (N1Ru-1)

Background

The Iglulualuit site was excavated by the author during the summer of 1987. It is located a few kilometers north of the mouth of the Horton River, on the western coast of Franklin Bay. Topography in this area is dominated by the Smoking Hills, so-called because of spontaneous combustion which has been active since at least 1826 (Franklin 1971: 231), and probably far longer (see Mackay 1958: 21-23). They are steep, silty hills reaching a height of about 150 metres, running north-south along the eastern coast of the Cape Bathurst peninsula. At some time in the fairly recent past, Mackay now suggests about A.D. 1600 (personal communication 1987, cf. Mackay 1981), the Horton River broke through the barrier of these hills to empty into Franklin Bay, leaving the semi-stagnant Old Horton Channel to meander into the sea on the western side of the peninsula at Harrowby Bay. The new Horton mouth has produced a sizeable delta, with an outer edge of low sand islands sweeping north several kilometers in a great arch. Inland, at the foot of the Smoking Hills, is a flat colluvial plain about 700 metres wide. Between the deltaic islands and the plain is a shallow tidal inlet, along the inland side of which is the Iglulualuit site.

Iglulualuit is one of the largest archaeological sites known from the Canadian Arctic. The name, which is traditional (Stefansson 1913: end map; 1914a: 308), means "many houses," and was even transferred to the Horton River ("Iglulualuit Kuuga" or "River of Many Houses"; see Nuligak 1966: frontispiece). It comprises the collapsed and partially buried ruins of at least 30 winter houses, distributed over an 800 m length of coast. Many of the houses are barely visible, and others have probably been entirely buried in the slow accumulation of colluvial silts

CHAPTER 2: THE SITES

FIGURE 3
THE IGLULUALUIT SITE

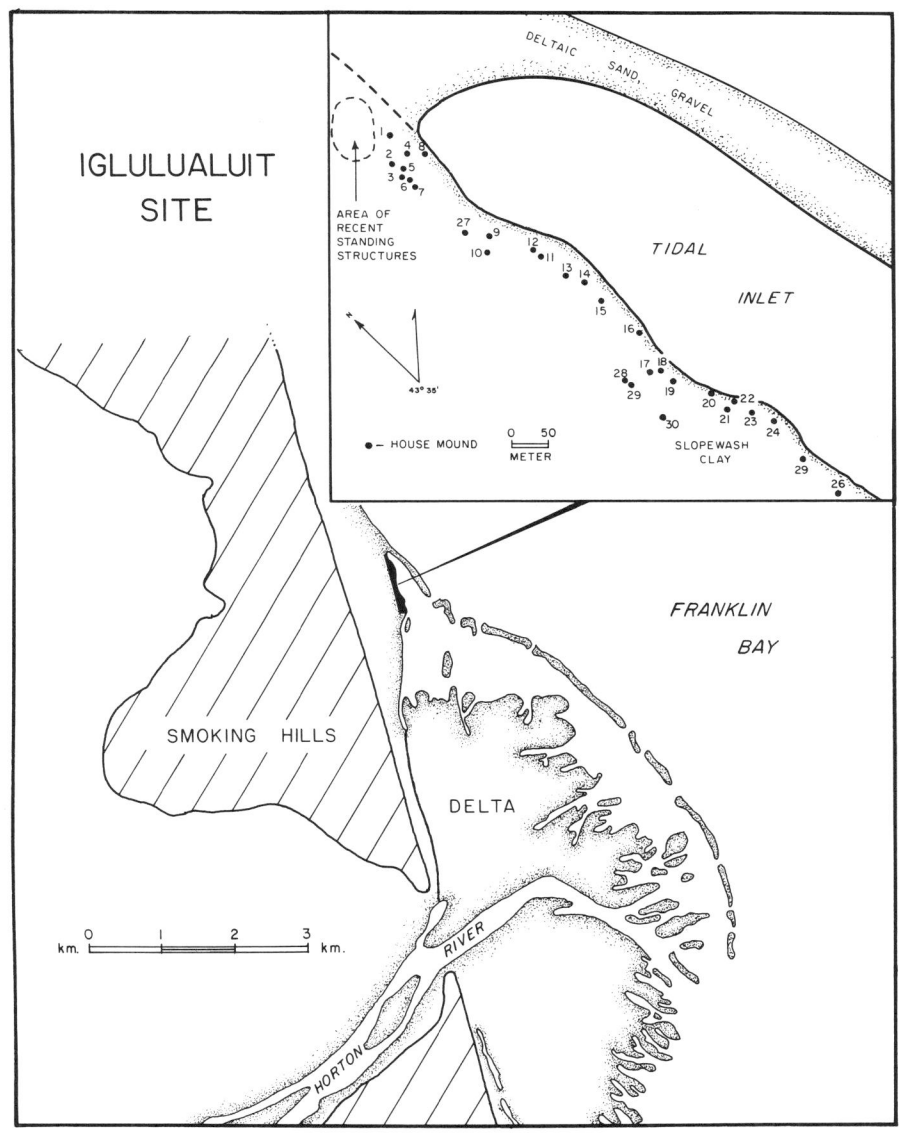

IGLULUALUIT PREHISTORY

FIGURE 4

Caribou Herd at Iglulualuit: "The soil was clayey, and from the recent thaw wet and soft. Tufts of the beautiful phlox ... were scattered over these, otherwise unsightly wastes; and, notwithstanding the scanty vegetation, rein-deer were numerous."

washed down from the Smoking Hills. As Richardson described the site area in July of 1826, "The soil was clayey, and from the recent thaw wet and soft. Tufts of the beautiful phlox, before mentioned, were scattered over these, otherwise unsightly wastes; and, notwithstanding the scanty vegetation, rein-deer were numerous" (in Franklin 1971: 231).

CHAPTER 2: THE SITES

The site was first noted by Stefansson around 1911 (Stefansson 1913: 368; 1914a: 308, 352), during the course of the Stefansson-Anderson Arctic Expedition. It has also been mentioned by Chipman and Cox (1924: 42) of the Canadian Arctic Expedition, and by Ross Mackay (1958: 116). Sometime before 1920, a trading post was established by Fritz Wolki at the northern end of the site (Chipman and Cox 1924: 42; Usher 1971: 108), presently represented by several partially-standing housepit dwellings. DEW-line construction in the 1950s at nearby Mallock Hill has resulted in the accumulation of a great deal of modern garbage and several standing frame buildings, again at the northern end of the site.

Some small-scale archaeological work had already been accomplished prior to the present excavations. In about 1911, Stefansson's colleague R. M. Anderson dug a small test pit, apparently in the middle of what is here called House 10 (see Fig. 3) (Stefansson 1913: 368). It produced a handful of artifacts, which are included in the artifact descriptions below. In 1986, Raymond LeBlanc visited the site as part of the Northern Oil and Gas Action Plan (NOGAP) archaeological assessment of the greater Mackenzie Delta region. He surface collected nine artifacts (LeBlanc 1987: 121-125), which again are included in this study.

It was apparent even prior to excavation that Iglulualuit was a comparatively recent site. From its location, Mackay (1958: 116) suggested it was unlikely to pre-date the Horton River

IGLULUALUIT PREHISTORY

breakthrough, which implies an age of less than about 400 years if his dating of that event is correct. As well, Stefansson reports that people living at Baillie Island in the early 20th century retained a memory of the community at Iglulualuit (Stefansson 1914a: 308, 352). Nonetheless, Iglulualuit was apparently abandoned by 1826. Richardson, who was normally very conscientious about noting Inuit villages (see Franklin 1971: 189-192, 208, 215, 230), failed to notice any standing structures at Iglulualuit, although he sailed by close enough to see two native tents (Franklin 1971: 232). These tents belonged to the "last Esquimaux seen" on his voyage east, cited above.

Excavations

The 1987 excavations at Iglulualuit were conducted over a six-week period, with a crew of three assistants. Work concentrated on two sod and driftwood houses, located far from the recent disturbances at the northern end of the site. They appear on the site map as Houses 11 and 20. Before excavation both houses appeared as shallow, roughly circular depressions, eight to ten metres in diameter, with few visible structural elements.

Excavation was greatly hampered by the clay/silt matrix in which the site as a whole is slowly being buried. Permafrost was high in the ground, but it was melt-water which ultimately became an intractable problem. As excavation proceeded the house pits slowly filled with water, which even when baled left behind a

CHAPTER 2: THE SITES

FIGURE 5

De-sodding House 20; the Smoking Hills are in the background.

heavy wet clay, obscuring cultural features and making architectural details very difficult to perceive. Rain finally filled one house entirely, while heavy mud made the second impossible to excavate much below the level of the sleeping platforms. Floor boards could only be felt through several centimeters of standing water. As well, it became evident that both houses had been badly damaged by ice rafting. Beyond broken vertical posts, there were few in situ roofing or wall elements in either structure.

IGLULUALUIT PREHISTORY

FIGURE 6

HOUSE 20, FLOOR PLAN

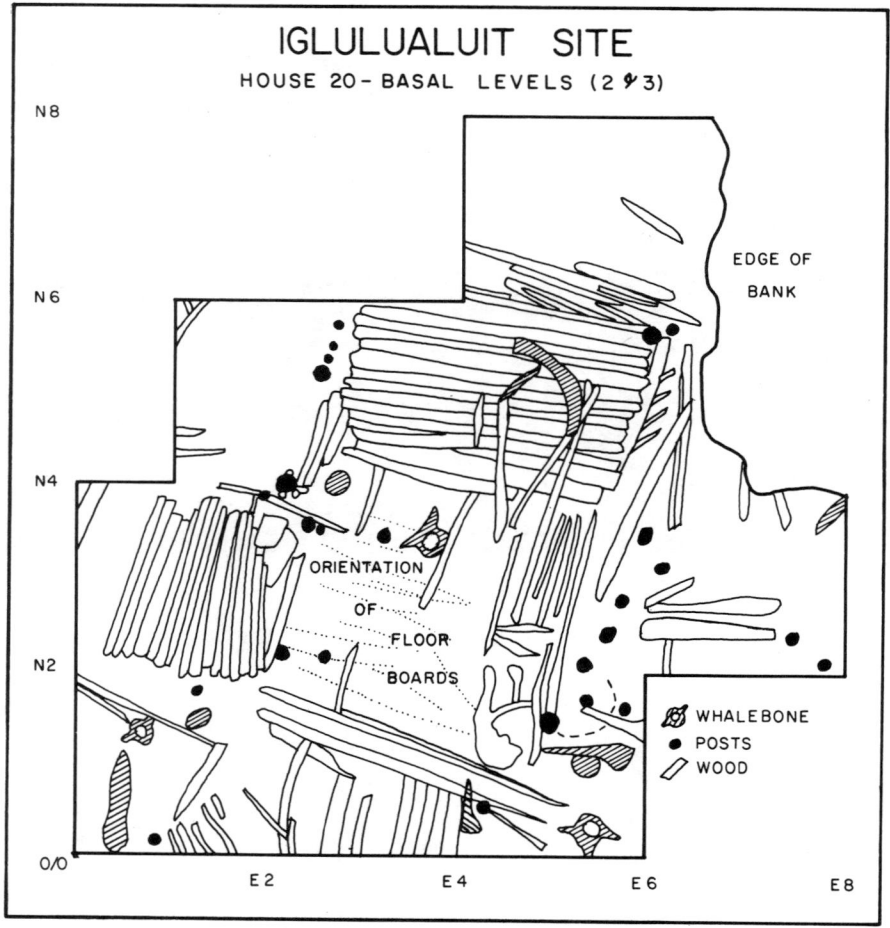

Nonetheless, something of the architecture can be described. Both houses were made largely of driftwood logs and poles, augmented by the occasional bowhead whale mandible or rib, rocks, and whale vertebrae. Both probably had a cold-trap entrance on the seaward side, but in the case of House 11 high ground-water

CHAPTER 2: THE SITES

FIGURE 7

HOUSE 11, FLOOR PLAN

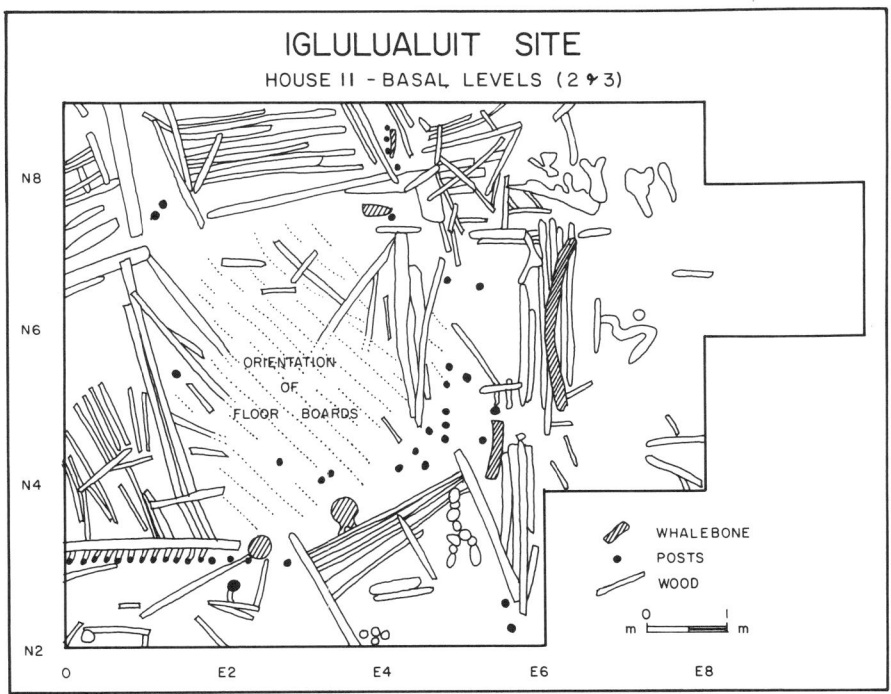

made excavation impossible, while in House 20 the passage had been destroyed by coastal erosion. Floors were recessed about 40 cmbelow present ground level and, although never clearly revealed, were apparently made of logs adzed flat on at least their upper surface. House 20 had the best preserved interior (Fig. 6), and clearly exhibits two sleeping platforms composed of parallel poles laid on a surface about 20 cm higher than the house floor. One of these platforms is opposite the presumed door, while the other is

IGLULUALUIT PREHISTORY

at right angles to it. A third possible platform is badly disturbed, but is situated on the fourth side of the square, making a cruciform-shaped structure. House 11 appears to have been similar, although only two platforms were revealed (Fig. 7). The interior area of House 20 is estimated at about 27 square-metres, exclusive of the entrance passage. The sleeping platforms have a total width of about eight metres, with each between 2 and 3.5 m wide. Ethnographic information suggests about half a metre of platform width per person (see McGhee 1984a: 80), in turn suggesting the house accommodated three nuclear families of up to seven people, one per platform. House 11 may have been slightly larger.

Faunal Material

Animal bones accounted for the great majority of items recovered from the Iglulualuit excavations, with House 11 producing 2847 specimens and House 20 2198, for a total faunal assemblage of 5045 specimens. Minimum Number of Individual (MNI) and Number of Identified Specimen (NISP) counts by smallest taxon are presented in Table 1. Bowhead whale bone has been excluded, since it is not clear that it represents a food source used at the site, or simply an architectural resource, scavenged or brought in from killing locations elsewhere. An indication of its relative frequency can be determined from the house floor plans. Fragmentary human remains of two individuals (one old person and

CHAPTER 2: THE SITES

one very young one, sex indeterminate) from the north sleeping platform of House 20 are also excluded.

Material from both houses is similar. Both are dominated by the remains of ringed seal (Phoca hispida), which make up between 80% and 90% of NISPs, and 36% to 38% of MNIs. Other sea mammals (Erignathus barbatus and Delphinapterus leucas) are quite rare. The most common terrestrial species by NISP count is caribou (Rangifer tarandus), followed by arctic and/or red fox (Alopex lagopus and Vulpes vulpes), an order which is reversed when considering MNIs. Foxes, then, are one group which show a much higher relative MNI than NISP frequency; possible indirect evidence of a non-food use. Birds in general are comparatively unimportant, with the minor exception of ptarmigan (Lagopus sp.), and fish bone was very rare indeed.

These figures are not atypical of coastal Inuit sites, which generally are dominated by either caribou, ringed seal or, around the mouth of the Mackenzie, beluga (see Morrison 1983a: 243; McGhee 1974: 34-35). A useful comparison, however, can be made with faunal frequencies from the historic Mackenzie Inuit site of Kugaluk (Morrison 1988a: 62-67), the nearest archaeological site for which detailed faunal information is available. The Kugaluk fauna was heavily dominated by caribou, with no evidence whatsoever of ringed seal. As well, fish and waterfowl were relatively important. These sharp differences are to some extent due to local environmental conditions, but probably relate more

TABLE 1

IGLULUALUIT FAUNAL MATERIAL

Taxon	House 11 NISP	%	MNI	%	House 20 NISP	%	MNI	%
MAMMALS								
Phoca hispida (ringed seal)	1507	80.72	28	37.3	1520	89.16	23	36.5
Rangifer tarandus (caribou)	162	8.68	3	4.0	35	2.05	2	3.2
Fox sp.	26	1.39	2	2.7	17	1.00	4	6.3
Alopex lagopus (Arctic fox)	21	1.12	7	9.3	25	1.47	6	9.5
Vulpes vulpes (red fox)	9	0.48	1	1.3	2	0.12	1	1.6
Spermophilus parryii (Arctic ground squirrel)	19	1.02	3	4.0	17	1.00	4	6.3
Canis sp.					11	0.64	2	3.2
Canis familiaris (dog)	19	1.02	3	4.0				
Erignathus barbatus (bearded seal)	8	0.43	1	1.3	3	0.18	1	1.6
Ursus sp. (bear)	2	0.11	1	1.3	6	0.35	1	1.6
Ovibos moschatus (musk-ox)	2	0.11	1	1.3	1	0.06	1	1.6
Alces alces (moose)	1	0.05	1	1.3	2	0.12	1	1.6
Alces/Ovibos					2	0.12		
Dicrostonyx torquatus (collared lemming)					1	0.06	1	1.6
Martes americana (marten)	1	0.05	1	1.3				
Ondatra zibethicus (muskrat)	1	0.05	1	1.3				
Delphinapterus leucas (beluga)	1	0.05	1	1.3				
unidentified	863				392			
BIRDS								
Lagopus sp.	34	1.82	5	6.7	50	2.93	8	12.7
Duck sp.	8	0.43			2	0.12		
Somateria mollissima (common eider)	2	0.11	1	1.3	1	0.06	1	1.6
Aythya valisineria (canvasback)	1	0.05	1	1.3				
Anas acuta (pintail)	1	0.05	1	1.3				
Melanitta deglandi (white-winged scoter)	1	0.05	1	1.3	2	0.12	2	3.2
Clangula hyemalis (oldsquaw)	1	0.05	1	1.3	1	0.06	1	1.6

TABLE 1 (Continued)

Taxon	House 11 NISP	%	MNI	%	House 20 NISP	%	MNI	%
Goose sp.	16	0.86			2	0.12	1	1.6
Branta bernicla (brant)	5	0.27	2	2.7				
Anser albifrons (white-fronted goose)	4	0.21	1	1.3				
Chen caerulescens (blue goose)	3	0.16	1	1.3				
Larus hyperboreus (glaucous gull)	4	0.21	1	1.3	2	0.12	1	1.6
Aquila chrysaëtos (golden eagle)	3	0.16	1	1.3				
Swan sp.	1	0.05	1	1.3	2	0.12		
Olor columbianus (whistling swan)					1	0.06	1	1.6
Stercorarius longicaudus (long-tailed jaeger)	1	0.05	1	1.3				
Stercorarius parasiticus (parasitic jaeger)	1	0.05	1	1.3				
Gavia arctica (Arctic loon)	1	0.05	1	1.3				
Scolopacidae (sandpiper)	1	0.05	1	1.3	1	0.06	1	1.6
Nyctea scandiaca (snowy owl)	1	0.05	1	1.3				
unidentified	114				25			
FISH (unidentified)	3				75			
Total Identified	1867	99.96	75	99.3	1706	100.10	63	101.7
Grand Total	2847				2198			

IGLULUALUIT PREHISTORY

specifically to the different place each site occupied in the seasonal subsistence round.

According to ethnohistorical and archaeological information, the more easterly Mackenzie Inuit (Nuvorugmiut and Avvaqmiut) spent the late summer/autumn period either hunting bowhead whales, or in the intensive pursuit of caribou. Seal hunting was important during the "dark days of winter", often with nets, when people lived in permanent driftwood houses in large coastal villages. Spring was generally spent in snow house communities on the sea ice, where breathing hole sealing was practiced (Richardson 1851: 257; Stefansson 1914a: 355-356; MacFarlane 1905: 681; Morrison 1988a). The Kugaluk occupation appears to have taken place over the summer-early winter period. It focussed primarily on the interception of the autumn caribou migration, and secondarily on fishing and waterfowl hunting. Both the nature of the site and the fauna suggest that Iglulualuit, by contrast, was a coastal, winter village, where sealing was the economic mainstay. The paucity of caribou bone, even though this animal is locally abundant in the summer, tends to support this contention.

This interpretation is in accord with the traditions of the Baillie Islanders, who recalled that Iglulualuit was an important seal netting location. Apparently the muddy waters of the Horton allowed the netting season to persist beyond the "dark days of winter" into the spring, when most of the people of Franklin Bay congregated at Iglulualuit to lay up a supply of oil and blubber

CHAPTER 2: THE SITES

(Stefansson 1914a: 352). It is unclear, however, whether the abundant seal remains at Iglulualuit relate specifically to netting. No netting gear was recovered, while Stefansson (1914a: 351) reports that the Baillie Islanders observed a taboo by destroying the bones of netted seals by dumping them down a crack in the ice. Later, we are specifically informed that all such sealing taboos were also in effect at Iglulualuit (Ibid.: 352). The importance of sealing in the Iglulualuit economy might thus have been even greater than the faunal assemblage indicates.

The examination of dental thin-sections is a useful technique for determining a prey animal's season of death (Morrison 1983b, 1988a). Unfortunately, for reasons which are unclear, very few seal mandibles (or other head elements) were recovered from the Iglulualuit excavations. Out of a total MNI from both houses of 51 individual ringed seals, there are only five individuals represented by mandibles. First molar thin-sections from these mandibles were prepared by the Palaeoenvironmental Laboratory at the Archaeological Survey of Canada. Readings tend to cluster in the April-May period, supporting the suggestion of spring netting. However, it is not clear how representative these results might be.

Langton Bay

The archaeological site called here Langton Bay was found and excavated by Stefansson over a period of a few days in early

IGLULUALUIT PREHISTORY

July of 1911. Unfortunately, his notes on the excavation are brief and cryptic. While camped at Langton Bay, his diary for June 30 describes excavating two graves (Stefansson 1914a: 311). The next entry, for July 3, states:

> Archaeology. Took a walk two miles west along coast to glance at ruins. There are three or more house ruins, some of them barely distinguishable from accumulations of driftwood and some of them may be nothing but wave-deposited driftwood, on the sandspit that makes the first lagoon west of the harbor. There are also three or more at the east end of this sandspit on higher land. There are one or more graves east of and a little higher than these house ruins.... Near one house was a sled runner of western type. Ilav. (Ilavinirk, a west Alaskan Inupiat employed by Stefansson) found near one of these yesterday a piece of sled runner of antler. Collected also one broken sealing stool last night and saw one today

(Stefansson 1914a: 311- 312, brackets mine).

Stefansson seems to have dug sporadically at Langton Bay for about a month, leaving to go to Okat, and then returning around the end of July. Early in his work he comments, "The house site

CHAPTER 2: THE SITES

here seems barren. Apparently the people had the fortune not to die of starvation, for they seem to have taken away with them all their goods" (Stefansson 1914a: 312). Despite this, the present collection is quite extensive, especially considering the brevity of the excavation.

A note on the site in <u>My Life with the Eskimo</u> (Stefansson 1913: 329) presents what little architectural information is available.

> There are a number of old house ruins on the sand spit which forms the outer wall of the Langton Bay harbor. Although wood is abundant enough in these parts, most of the houses seem to have had their walls made of the bones of whales, especially of the vertebrae and skull bones. Although we did a considerable amount of work in digging out these dwellings, we found but few things of importance except pottery fragments...."

A final source of information on Langton Bay comes from the testimony of Panigyuk, Stefansson's Baillie Island informant, who was born in the Langton Bay area in the 1830s. According to her, the Langton Bay harbour sandspit (and hence presumably the village), was known as "Nuwuayuk." A nearby island called "kalit" ("sandspit") was formed when an umiak towing a whale ashore was

IGLULUALUIT PREHISTORY

seen by menstruating women "and boatmen and whale turned to sandspits" (Stefansson 1914a: 307). A nearby river mouth was an important spring sealing location, the animals being speared as they hauled up out of their breathing holes. People lived on whale, seal, caribou, and fish at different seasons. Net fishing, however, was unknown (Stefansson 1913: 332; 1914a: 332).

Artifacts from Langton Bay were generously loaned for this study by the American Museum of Natural History in New York, who sponsored the Stefansson-Anderson Expedition.

Okat ("Kugum Pana")

A second Franklin Bay site is located near Okat (or "Tomcod") Bay, at the mouth of an unnamed river northeast of Langton Bay, and behind Pt. Stivens. This river was an important portage route across the Cape Parry peninsula, allowing water transportation to within about a kilometre of Darnley Bay. According to Panigyuk, the site's native name was "Kugum pana" or "mouth of the river," but Stefansson and Wissler (1916) usually refer to it as Okat. It was evidently Panigyuk's home village, and some of the houses were still standing when she and her family left for Baillie Island in about 1840 (Stefansson 1913: 153, 328, 330-331; Stefansson 1914a: 307).

The Okat site was originally found by Stefansson's companion Ilavinirk (Stefansson 1913: 328), and Stefansson worked there during an interruption in his work at Langton Bay. His diary

CHAPTER 2: THE SITES

entry for July 7, 1911, states "Preparing to start for the river mouth north of Okat. Shall send men thence to get our cache in Darnley Bay by boat up the river, while I dig the ruins there" (Stefansson 1914a: 312). On July 10 he writes;

> Point Stivens. Archaeology. The house sites here seem very old. The best preserved rafters underground can easily be picked to pieces with the fingers, though ends that stick above the surface are harder. It seems not unlikely that the village has in part been carried off by the river, as Ilav. made most of his finds on the beach last year and this time we found specimens under water ten yards from the cutbank. The house we first attacked was half gone. Other houses are still intact, unless there be some that are completely gone.
>
> Our finds so far comprise several score specimens, none of which are perfect....
>
> The house first excavated appears to have been burnt down. Some of the timbers show no signs of fire and others only a little charring, but a few are burnt off so that only an eighteen or twenty inch stub remains. These seem to have been the

IGLULUALUIT PREHISTORY

> rafters. Such a fire in an Eskimo earth-and-wood house it seems must have been intentionally kindled, a mass of fuel being carried indoors and ignited. There are no human bones, nor in fact any other bones inside the house. On the roof have been fragments of caribou, swan, ptarmigan, squirrel, and other bones. There are scattered on the beach a few ribs of very small whales. Most of the things found seem to have been on the roof when it caved in.
>
> One lamp-place only could be definitely located by the oil soaked into the floor combined with flat stones on which the lamp evidently stood. This was on the right side of the door, in the corner (southwest corner, or rather south corner as house faced southeast). This is in conformity to Mackenzie custom.... (Stefansson 1914a: 313).

On July 11 he continues:

> Archaeology. Started on the second house today, the largest and most westerly. All the other houses face southeast, but this faced north, the end of the alleyway being

CHAPTER 2: THE SITES

> already cut off by the river. What remained of the alleyway was about six feet long by three feet wide. The house is the usual "round cornered rectangle" the transverse diameters are approximately five m., twenty cm. by six m., ten cm.... (Stefansson 1914a: 313-314).

Excavation apparently continued until the 23rd of July, when Stefansson returned to Langton Bay (Stefansson 1913: 333). Generally, the state of preservation of the ruins convinced him of the considerable antiquity of the site, or at least of the portion of it he was excavating. He did not doubt Panigyuk's account, but suggested that the more recent sections of the village had been destroyed by the river (Stefansson 1913: 331).

Most of the Okat collection is the property of the American Museum of Natural History, who again generously provided it on loan. The Archaeological Survey of Canada (Canadian Museum of Civilization) also has material which apparently comes from the site. Catalogue records give the provenance as "Old House Ruin, S.E. Corner Franklin Bay, Arctic Ocean, Can.", and attribute it to V. Stefansson, "on expedition." This is very similar to the American Museum of Natural History catalogue reference for Okat; "From an old house ruin near Okat, fishing place, S.E. corner Franklin Bay, Arctic Ocean, Canada, July, 1911." Much of this

IGLULUALUIT PREHISTORY

Archaeological Survey of Canada collection consists of debitage, but it does contain a few dozen tools which are included in the artifact descriptions in the following chapters. Even with this addition, however, the Okat collection is relatively sparse, an observation at odds with Stefansson's (1913: 333) description of Okat as a "very rich village site." There are few discrepancies between the collection as it now stands, and that described by Wissler (1916) soon after it arrived in New York. Apparently, however, some of the collection did not make it South because of transportation problems (see Wissler 1916: 417).

The sites information data base of the Archaeological Survey of Canada, Canadian Museum of Civilization, has a record for a site designated NjRp-1, located "at the base of a small peninsula extending into Tom Cod Bay on the W. side of Parry Peninsula." It consists of five house mounds and a number of tent circles, and was seen from the air by S.C. Zoltai (Northern Forest Research Centre, Edmonton), in 1978. It is probably the Okat site.

Booth Island

The Booth Island site is located west of Cape Parry, on Booth Island. It was excavated by John Hadley, a member of the Canadian Arctic Expedition of 1913 to 1918. Hadley had been a fur trapper and trader at Cape Smythe, Alaska, when he joined the Expedition in 1913, in time to be aboard the ill-fated _Karluk_ when it was caught and crushed in the ice off north Alaska (McKinlay

CHAPTER 2: THE SITES

1976). He survived the winter on Wrangle Island, and re-joined the expedition at Herschel in 1915 (Stefansson 1921: 388), the only survivor of the Karluk to do so. He eventually became master of Stefansson's ship <u>Polar Bear</u>. Notes at the Archaeological Survey of Canada (Old Catalogue System) indicate that the site was excavated in 1917, and Stefansson's route map shows <u>Polar Bear</u> stopping at Booth Island in the summer of that year (Stefansson 1921: 763). Without more detailed information it is impossible to determine how long Hadley had to work at the site, but given the exigencies of the sailing season it could have only a brief period. He died the following year. The only other notes that survive, and probably the only ones taken, indicate that the collection was "found in ruins of old houses 1 ft. down" (ASC, Old Catalogue System).

Artifact Analysis

Artifacts from Iglulualuit, Langton Bay, Okat, and Booth Island are described and compared in the following chapters. External comparison centres on several regional variants of prehistoric Eskimo culture, from both east and west of Franklin Bay. The nearest are the Mackenzie Inuit, best known from Kittigazuit (McGhee 1974), with other sites including Pt. Atkinson (Mathiassen 1930), Kugaluk (Morrison 1988a), Barry (Morrison 1988b) Radio Creek (McGhee 1974), Bombadier Channel (Arnold 1986), and Cache Point (Stromberg 1987). All of these sites post-date

IGLULUALUIT PREHISTORY

A.D. 1400, with Radio Creek and Cache Creek being probably the earliest. The only Thule culture site from the Mackenzie Inuit area is Washout, on Herschel Island (Yorga 1980). It dates to before A.D. 1400, but its relationship to the development of Mackenzie Inuit culture is considered by the excavator to be problematic (see Yorga 1980: 132-136).

From western Alaska comes the sequence of dendrochronologically-dated Kobuk River sites, ranging in age from Ahteut (A.D. 1250) to Ambler Island (A.D. 1750) (Giddings 1952). Closely related are nearby coastal sites such as Nukleet (Giddings 1964) and Cape Krusenstern (Giddings and Anderson 1986), and interior sites like Kangiguksuk (Hall 1971). This west Alaskan sequence has recently been divided into an Early Thule phase (A.D. 900-1300), Late Thule, including Ekseavik (A.D. 1300-1400), and Kotzebue culture, dating after A.D. 1400 and including the Kotzebue sites and Ambler Island (Giddings and Anderson 1986). As McGhee (1974) has noted, there appears to have been a particularly strong connection between later west Alaskan material and the culture of the Mackenzie Inuit.

The Pt. Barrow area has seen considerable archaeological work; indeed Stefansson's excavations there in 1912 are among the earliest in the New World Arctic (Stefansson 1914a; Wissler 1916). The north Alaskan sequence includes a Thule phase, sometimes called Nunagiak (A.D. 900-1400), followed by a Recent or Utkiavik phase (Ford 1959; Stanford 1976).

CHAPTER 2: THE SITES

Analogues from the area east of Franklin Bay include Eastern or so-called Canadian Thule, defined in the Baffin Island-northwest Hudson Bay area (Mathiassen 1927b), a strongly western-influenced variant of Thule culture in the Coronation Gulf area (Morrison 1983a), and at least potentially, the culture of the late prehistoric and early historic Copper Inuit (Jenness 1946; McGhee 1972; Morrison 1981).

All of these cultural manifestations share a common origin in the development of Thule culture in northwestern Alaska about 1000 years ago, and exhibit a general similarity in most aspects of material culture. Comparison, therefore, focuses especially on a few diagnostic artifacts. For the most part, debitage and unidentified fragments are ignored.

Chapter 3
SEA MAMMAL HUNTING GEAR
IGLULUALUIT

Harpoon and Dart Heads

Twelve finished harpoon heads were recovered. All but one can be classed as Nuwuk type (Ford 1959: 93); "thin," with a closed socket, a lateral spur, and a blade slit parallel to the line hole (Pl. 1, a-e, g). All but one has a rivet hole to secure the endblade, and all are made of antler. None show any decoration, but one (Pl. 1, g) exhibits the short spur and blunt tip outline which seems characteristic of similar heads from Kittigazuit (McGhee 1974: Pl. 7,a; Pl. 14,a; Pl. 18,a; Pl. 21,a). Two have bone endblades still in place. Discounting them, overall lengths range from 51.5 to 70 mm. The collection also includes a blank and three distal blade prongs which probably represent the Nuwuk type.

The only other finished harpoon head can be classified as Kotzebue type 1 (Giddings 1952: 53). It is self-bladed, with a pair of opposite barbs parallel to the line hole, a closed socket, and a symmetrical spur (Pl. 1, h). It is made of antler, and is 61.5 mm long; about the same size as the Nuwuk heads. Again, ornamentation is absent.

A final type present at Iglulualuit is represented by a whale bone blank 94 mm long (Pl. 1, i). It appears to be of the Nunagiak barbed type (Ford 1959: 87), which is similar to Kotzebue type 1, except that the barbs are at right angle to the line hole. The socket has not yet been cut, but from the thickness of the proximal end a closed socket seems to have been intended.

What are here termed **dart heads** differ from harpoon heads in having a male tang for attachment to a shaft or socketpiece, rather than the female socket seen on toggling harpoon heads. A whale bone specimen is 232 mm long (Pl. 1, f). The distal end is cut flat and was in the process of being reworked when lost or

CHAPTER 3: SEA MAMMAL HUNTING GEAR

abandoned, while the shoulderless, conical tang is polished as if from use. There is a single strong lateral barb, set off by incised lines on either face. The line hole is drilled and laterally placed.

Other Harpoon Parts

Harpoon **endblades** were made of both bone and ground stone (Pl. 1, j-n). Of five loose bone specimens, three have drilled rivet holes to match those on the blade prongs of the Nuwuk harpoon heads, while the remaining two are fragmentary. Outlines are ovate, or sub-triangular, with straight bases. One specimen has pronounced lateral "ears," while all are basally thinned or fluted to accommodate narrow blade slits. Lengths range from 39 to 54 mm.

Two of the four stone endblades are complete. One has a broad, leaf-shaped outline, with a straight base and some basal thinning. The other has a square base and a narrow, tapering tip. Lengths are 44 and 41.5 mm, respectively. The broken specimens show a medial ridge in one case, and fairly pronounced basal thinning in the other. None of the stone specimens is drilled for a securing rivet.

The tip of an antler **foreshaft** has a round cross-section, fitting closed socket harpoon heads like those described. It is too fragmentary for further description.

A single antler fragment may represent Mathiassen's (1927b: 34) Type 2 **socketpiece**; a hollow antler tube which acted as a sleeve to reinforce the shaft of a very light throwing harpoon. There is a double lashing groove around one end.

Miscellaneous

A heavy wooden toggle handle may have functioned as a seal **drag-handle** for ice hunting. It is cylindrical, 68 mm long and 36 mm in cross-section, with a deeply recessed central lashing bed

IGLULUALUMIUT PREHISTORY

(Pl. 36, c).

A broken tool made on a long metatarsal splinter has a blunt, conical distal end. The cross-section above is triangular, and the whole piece shows use-polish. The distal working end exhibits multiple striae running around the circumference, superficially suggesting use as a drill. However, close examination indicates the striae are discontinuous and not always parallel, and are probably the result of the manufacturing technique. Similar specimens from north and west Alaska have been called **"gauged drills"**, and have the suggested function of removing ice and snow from harpoon head line holes (Giddings 1952: 54-55; 1964: 62; Stanford 1976: 59). Alternatively, Hall (1971: 42) has identified Brooks Range specimens as true drills, while Mackenzie Inuit examples from Kittigazuit have been tentatively described as foreshafts (McGhee 1974: 46).

Langton Bay

Harpoon Heads

A comparison of the present Langton Bay harpoon head collection and that described by Wissler (1916: 418) suggests that at least two specimens are now missing. The present sample comprises seventeen heads representing five different types. As at Iglulualuit, by far the most common is the Nuwuk closed socket type, with 13 specimens ranging in length from about 54 to 90 mm (Pl. 2, a-k). All are made of antler, and with one exception all are plain. This decorated specimen has a Y-motif incised over the line hole on both faces, flanked on either side by a single line. All but one harpoon head has a rivet hole for the endblade, and in one case part of the bone endblade is still in place. Three specimens exhibit a lashing groove around the outside of the base to strengthen the socket. Many are rather roughly finished compared to similar specimens from Iglulualuit, in that the edges of the line of small drilled holes used to cut the endblade slit

CHAPTER 3: SEA MAMMAL HUNTING GEAR

have not been smoothed flat. One of the missing harpoon heads was also apparently of Nuwuk type, and had an ivory endblade still in place. There are also two blanks in the collection which suggest the Nuwuk type.

Other types are represented by single specimens. A whalebone head is of the Brower type (Ford 1959: 90), with a closed socket, a lateral spur, two opposite barbs, and an endblade slit cut parallel to the line hole (Pl. 2, m). It is 112.5 mm long, and has a small, sharp point or nipple on each shoulder, just above the line hole. It is otherwise plain. A broken antler harpoon head (Pl. 2, o) represents the Clachan closed socket type; thin, barbless, with a closed socket, a lateral spur, and an endblade slit at right-angles to the line hole (Morrison 1983a: 80). Another (Pl. 2, n) is of the Clachan open socket type, which is similar except in having an open socket (Morrison 1983a: 76). Another is the distal end of a Thule type 2 harpoon head (Mathiassen 1927b: 15), broken just below the line hole (Pl. 2, l). It has a drilled hole at the tip, suggesting it may be an old specimen, worn as an amulet (cf. Murdoch 1892: 219-220). It has a point or spur on each shoulder like the Brower specimen. A final harpoon head from Langton Bay is now missing, but illustrated by Wissler (1916: Fig. 22). It is of Thule type 1 (Mathiassen 1927b: 14), having neither barbs nor an inserted blade, and an open socket with drilled lashing holes, and a lateral spur. It was found on the surface, and was 118 mm long.

Other Harpoon Parts

A single harpoon **endblade** is made of bone, with a rivet hole and a trianguloid shape (Pl. 2, p). The edges have distinct grinding facets, and it has been centrally thinned or fluted. It is 45 mm long.

Three whale bone **foreshafts** are 290 to 310 mm long, slightly curved, with narrow, ovate cross-sections, and a "loose," conical

IGLULUALUMIUT PREHISTORY

base (Pl. 3, a-b). The distal ends are blunt and designed to articulate with closed-socket harpoon heads. Each has a drilled, laterally-placed hole which would have secured a line to prevent loss (see Mason 1902: Fig. 83), and they are long and narrow enough to have been used in breathing-hole sealing (cf. Murdoch 1892: Fig. 227). A quite different type of foreshaft is made of ivory. It is only 123 mm long, with a wedge-shaped "fixed" proximal end (Pl. 3, c).

There are two harpoon **socketpieces**, both of which would have been used with conically based, loose foreshafts. One is made of ivory, 186 mm long, and represents Mathiassen's (1927b: 33) Type 1 (Pl. 3, e). It has a wedge-shaped proximal end, with a lashing hole. Above this the cross-section is nearly round, and the slightly bulbous distal end is equipped with a conical socket hole. Murdoch describes nearly identical socketpieces of about the same size and weight, used with a very short foreshaft to make a medium-weight throwing harpoon used for seal (Murdoch 1892: 230). A much heavier whale bone socketpiece is 224 mm long, and might have been used for beluga (Pl. 3, d). It has straight sides, a round cross-section and a blunt, conical tang set below slight shoulders. It is encircled by four raised lines towards the base, and pierced by a lashing hole. The conical socket hole would accommodate only a very heavy shaft.

Sealing Stool

Stefansson (1914a: 312) mentions collecting a stealing stool from Langton Bay, but it has not apparently survived. Sealing stools were used in breathing-hole seal hunting (see Murdoch 1892: 255).

Lance Head

A small antler lance head is 67 mm long (Pl. 2, q). It is flat, with a roughened, wedge-shaped base, and an endblade slit

CHAPTER 3: SEA MAMMAL HUNTING GEAR

cut through the width of the rounded distal end. The blade slit is equipped with a rivet hole, and there is a small hole drilled near one margin of the tang, presumably to hold a lashing. It has a lenticular cross-section 13 mm wide. So small a specimen would presumably have been used in the kayak hunting of small seals or caribou.

Okat

Harpoon and Dart Heads

One small harpoon head is of the Nuwuk type, like those Iglulualuit and Langton Bay. It is 65.5 mm long, and made of antler, plain, and with a rivet hole for the endblade (Pl. 4,c). The blade slit again has been formed with a drill, and then roughly cut out. A second closed-socket harpoon head is made of whale bone, and is considerably larger (length: 89 mm). It has a lenticular cross-section, compared with the ovate or nearly round cross-section of typical Nuwuk heads, no rivet hole, and a line hole flanked on either side by a vertical incised line (Pl. 4,b). It might be said to represent the Barrow type, a larger and usually decorated variant of Nuwuk (Ford 1959: 92-93).

A **whaling harpoon head** was recovered from Okat, and briefly described by Wissler (1916: 418), but is now missing. It had a closed socket, a drilled line hole placed toward one lateral margin, and an endblade slit at right-angles to the line hole. The total length appears to have been about 210 mm.

A slender whale bone **dart head** 340 mm long has a shoulderless conical base, a laterally-placed line hole, and three unilateral barbs (Pl. 4,a). The distal end is slit for an endblade.

Other Harpoon Parts

A single triangular slate **endblade** has sharply bevelled edges and no rivet hole (Pl. 4,h). There is no evidence of basal

IGLULUALUMIUT PREHISTORY

thinning or fluting.

Loose whale bone **foreshafts** are identical to the long, narrow form described from Langton Bay; one nearly complete specimen is 290 mm long (Pl. 4, g). A different kind of foreshaft is short (length: 116.5 mm), with an expanded and thinned proximal end which has been roughened for fixed attachment (Pl. 4, k). It loosely resembles the short, fixed foreshaft from Langton Bay.

Two Type 1 **socketpieces** are both made of whale bone (Pl. 4, i). They are broken, but are complete as to their lengths, which range from 197 to 212 mm. Bases are wedge-shaped, with a very slight shoulder in one case, above which is a lashing hole. This same specimen has a slightly expanded distal end, while the other is straight-sided. An unusual socketpiece is again made of whale bone, but is very short (61.5 mm), with a wedge-shaped shoulderless tang (Pl. 4, j). It is not clear that it is for a harpoon, although the deep, conical socket fits the loose foreshafts in the collection fairly well.

Lance Heads

Antler lance heads similar to the Langton Bay specimen were recovered, with lengths ranging from 87 to 99.5 mm (Pl. 4, d-f). They are flat, with rounded distal ends slit through the greatest width for an endblade, and equipped with a rivet hole. The form of the tang element varies; one specimen has a split base, one is of pyramidal form, and two have wedge bases, in all cases equipped with one or more lashing holes. The tang element is slightly shouldered, and roughened for attachment.

Miscellaneous

A small, plain antler toggle may be a **drag handle** (Pl. 4, l).

CHAPTER 3: SEA MAMMAL HUNTING GEAR

Booth Island

Harpoon and Dart Heads

The Booth Island site produced a total of 81 harpoon heads. In contrast to the harpoon heads from other Franklin Bay sites, almost all are of open socket "Thule" types. Most are made of antler, with only a few examples made of whale bone.

The most numerous are Thule type 2 (Pl. 5, a-j), the most common and distinctive of Thule culture harpoon heads. Of 29 specimens, seven are distal fragments, and three others are broken off just below the line hole. The remainder include two with a groove or bed to hold the lashing around the open socket, eight with drilled lashing holes, and nine with lashing slots. Most have a fairly well defined shoulder at or slightly above the level of the line hole, with incised lines defining a lateral ridge on either margin, running from the shoulder to the base. One unusual characteristic is a raised point or nipple at the point of the shoulder, seen on eight specimens. Spurs are usually smoothly cut in the case of specimens with lashing slots, and angled in specimens with drilled lashing holes. Barbs are opposite and two in number, with one multi-barbed exception. Several show very cunning repairs. Decoration is limited to a Y-motif or filled triangle incised over the line hole on most specimens. Lengths range from 67 to 157 mm.

Nearly as common are Thule type 3 specimens (Mathiassen 1927b: 18), of which there are 28 (Pl. 5, k-q). Twenty-two have drilled lashing holes, and only six have slotted holes. All but two of the former also have rivet holes for the endblade, while all but two of the latter lack them. Most specimens are plain, with only a few exhibiting a Y-motif over the line hole, sometimes flanked by vertical incised lines. Lengths range from about 70 mm, to 118 mm. Two specimens tend toward the apparently early Sicco sub-type (Ford 1959: 83), with flattened facial facets and lateral constrictions at about the level of the line hole, wherein are set

IGLULUALUMIUT PREHISTORY

vestigial or ornamental sideblade slots (Pl. 5, k-l). One is further decorated with a Y-motif and flanking incised lines on both faces. Both, however, exhibit such anomolously late characteristics as drilled lashing holes and/or a rivet hole for the endblade.

The Clachan open socket type (Morrison 1983a: 76) is represented by at least eight examples (Pl. 6, a-f). This type resembles Thule type 2, except that instead of being self-barbed it is equipped with a slot for an endblade, perpendicular to the line hole. It shares the long neck, well-defined shoulders, and lateral ridges of Thule type 2, and three examples also illustrate the unusual shoulder point or nipple seen on Thule type 2s from this site. Only two have slotted lashing holes, while one of the specimens with drilled lashing holes has a strongly scalloped spur (Pl. 6, f). This is usually considered to be an early trait, reminiscent of the double-spurs seen on Birnirk harpoon heads (Ford 1959: 82), so it is noteworthy that it is once again associated with a "late" style of lashing attachment. Decoration is sparse, limited to the occasional Y-motif incised over the line hole. Lengths range from about 82 to 113 mm. A further eight proximal fragments may represent either Clachan open socket or Thule type 2. Three have drilled lashing holes, five have slots, and two have shoulder points.

Two fragmentary open socket harpoon heads differ from the above in being "flat" rather than "thin" (see Mathiassen 1927b: 12), in having two dorsal spurs and, in at least one case, two transverse line holes (Pl. 6, g-h). One has lashing slots, and the other drilled holes. They appear to represent Mathiassen's (1927b: 22) B1a type, or something closely similar.

Five harpoon heads have closed shaft sockets, and can be classed as either Nuwuk or Barrow type (Pl. 6, i-l). Two are broken and very small (estimated about 57 mm long), and two others are somewhat longer (about 85 mm). All four are identical to

CHAPTER 3: SEA MAMMAL HUNTING GEAR

"Nuwuk" specimens from Iglulualuit, Langton Bay and Okat, with endblade rivet holes and an absence of decoration. A final specimen, although broken, was evidently significantly larger (perhaps 110 mm long; Pl. 6, 1). It exhibits incised decoration in the form of an elaborated Y-motif over the line hole, flanked on either side by a pair of vertical lines running from the tip to the base. It might be said to represent the Barrow type.

A broken whale bone **dart head** has an extant length of 153 mm, and resembles the specimen from Iglulualuit (Pl. 7, e). It has a conical tang, a laterally-placed, slotted line hole, and a single extant barb. A spurred line adjacent to the barb on either face may be an ownership mark, or simply decoration.

Other Harpoon Parts

Nine trianguloid harpoon **endblades** are all made of ground slate (Pl. 6, m-n). Corners tend to be rounded and bases slightly concave, with several specimens showing a pronounced basal-interior thinning. Most edges were ground without facets, and none have been pierced for a rivet. Complete lengths range from 25 to 50 mm.

A complete antler **foreshaft** is straight and comparatively short (152 mm long), with a conical "loose" proximal end and a medially-placed, slotted line hole (Pl. 7, a). Three other broken specimens (Pl. 7, b) seem to be of a similar shape, and also have medial line holes, two drilled and one slotted. All are decorated with an incised Y-motif.

The tubular or type 2 style of **socketpiece** is represented by one nearly complete specimen, with a lashing groove around one end (Pl. 7, c). It is made of antler, with an outside diameter of 23.5 mm, and a length of 117 mm. A fragmentary example may have been similar.

IGLULUALUMIUT PREHISTORY

Lance Head

A lance head similar to specimens from Langton Bay and Okat is made of whale bone (Pl. 6, o). It has an endblade slit cut through the plane of greatest width, and a wedge-shaped tang with serrated edges. The blade slit is provided with a rivet hole, and the total length is 80 mm.

Miscellaneous

Four antler **wound pins** all have diamond-shaped cross-sections and a recessed bed beneath the expanded head (Pl. 7, f-i). Lengths range from 88 to 143.5 mm.

A whale bone pencil 210 mm long has a diameter of only 4.5 mm. It comes to a blunt point at one end, and has a slotted hole for the attachment of a line at the other (Pl. 7, d). It strongly resembles the kind of breathing-hole **seal indicator** regularly used by historic Central Eskimo (Jenness 1946: Fig. 145), and occasionally by Western Eskimo (Murdoch 1892: 254). This is the first such specimen to be reported from a Thule culture context (see Mathiassen 1927b: 42).

An unfinished **drag handle** is made of whale bone, and is 88 mm long (Pl. 7, j). Evidently, animal-head terminals were planned, as the ears (of a bear?) are roughly indicated. The central hole has not yet been drilled. It is a much more elaborate handle than the simple wooden specimen found at Iglulualuit.

Discussion

A major distinction can be made between the open socket harpoon heads which characterize the Booth Island collection, and the mainly closed socket heads found at Iglulualuit, Okat, and Langton Bay. This is of course a reflection of the Thule culture affiliation of Booth Island, while the other three sites were evidently occupied at a later date. The stylistic contrast

CHAPTER 3: SEA MAMMAL HUNTING GEAR

TABLE 2

Location of Sea Mammal Hunting Gear: Franklin Bay Sites

	Iglulualuit H 11	H 20	Misc.	Langton	Okat	Booth
Harpoon heads:						
closed socket: Kotzebue 1	1					
Nuwuk	7	1	3	14	1	4
Nuwuk, blank		1		2		
Barrow					1	1
Nunagiak barbed			1			
Brower				1		
Clachan closed				1		
open socket: Clachan open				1		8
Clachan/Thule 2						8
Thule 2				1		29
Thule 3						28
Thule 1				1		
B1a						2
Whaling harpoon head					1	
Dart heads		1			1	1
Harpoon endblades: bone	3	2		1		
stone	1	3			1	9
Foreshafts: short, "fixed"				1	1	
long, "loose"				3	3	
short, "loose"						4
fragment		1				
Harpoon socketpiece: Type 1				2	2	
Type 2	1					2
aberrant					1	
Sealing stool				1		
Lance heads				1	4	1
Wound Pins						4
Seal Indicator						1
Drag-line Handle		1			1	1
"Gauged drill"		1				

IGLULUALUMIUT PREHISTORY

between Recent and Thule assemblages is perhaps most clearly seen in this shift from open to closed socket harpoon heads, implicit in Mathiassen's (1927b) original definition of the open socket "Thule types."

The harpoon heads from Booth Island show important similarities with those from neighbouring Thule sites. The most common are "classic" Thule type 2s, with about an equal proportion of drilled and slotted lashing holes. Thule type 3, the next most abundant, includes specimens recalling the Sicco subtype, with lateral "waists" and ornamental sideblade slots. The Sicco variant of Thule type 3 is generally considered to be a very early time-marker (Taylor 1963), so it is perhaps surprising to find that all of the Booth Island specimens have either drilled lashing holes, or endblade rivet holes. Both of these are considered late traits, particularly in the Western Arctic (Collins 1937: 309). This combination of ornamental sideblade slots and drilled lashing and/or rivet holes is rare outside of the western Canadian Arctic, but common in Thule sites from western Coronation Gulf (Morrison 1983a) to Cape Parry (Taylor 1972). It also occurs on harpoon heads from the Maleraulik site on King William Island (Mathiassen 1927a: Pl. 82, fig. 2).

Clachan open socket harpoon heads are well represented at Booth Island, and show a similar geographic distribution to the Sicco-like Thule type 3s, from the Mackenzie River to western Coronation Gulf (see Morrison 1983a: 78). Several Clachan type specimens, and several of the Thule type 2s, also have sharp spurs or points on the shoulder, a trait shared with later Franklin Bay sites, and with, again, the Clachan site on western Coronation Gulf.

Another Booth Island harpoon head is the B1a type. Outside of the Eastern Arctic, similar specimens are found at Kittigazuit (McGhee 1974: 45) and the Thule culture Jackson site (Taylor 1972: Pl. II,d), which is located just east of Booth Island, at Cape Parry. Closed socket Barrow and Nuwuk harpoon heads also appear

CHAPTER 3: SEA MAMMAL HUNTING GEAR

in local Thule sites, such as Vaughan, Morris, and Clachan (Taylor 1972: Pl. 1,c; Pl. IV, b; Morrison 1983a: 92).

Turning to the Iglulualuit, Langton Bay, and Okat assemblages, the Nuwuk harpoon head type (including its larger Barrow analogue) predominates heavily, as it does in nearly all Recent assemblages from north and west Alaska (Giddings 1952, 1964; Giddings and Anderson 1986; Ford 1959; Stanford 1976), the Mackenzie Delta area (Mathiassen 1930; McGhee 1974; Morrison 1988a, 1988b), and well into the Central Arctic (Jenness 1946: Fig. 140; Morrison 1981: 262; J. Garth Taylor 1978: 85). Other types such as Brower and Nunagiak barbed are more specific to the Western Arctic, and can be duplicated in Mackenzie Inuit and Alaskan contexts (McGhee 1974: 45; Hall 1971: Pl. 7, fig. 14; Yorga 1980: 63; Ford 1959: 87-90; Mathiassen 1930: Pl. 1, fig. 5). Kotzebue type 1, found at Iglulualuit, is reported from late prehistoric western Alaskan sites like Intermediate Kotzebue (Giddings 1952: 53) and the Kotzebue culture beaches at Cape Krusenstern (Giddings and Anderson 1986: 45). Its north Alaskan counterpart is the Kilimatavik type (Ford 1959: 89).

Only Langton Bay produced a few harpoon heads which may be out of place in a late prehistoric site; Thule type 1, Thule type 2, Clachan open socket, and Clachan closed-socket specimens. Their presence could indicate either a transitional status for the site, or the presence of an earlier Thule component. Given the nature of the excavation and documentation, there is little to choose between these two alternatives. The presence of tiny spurs or points on the shoulders of long-necked harpoon heads such as Thule type 2 and the Clachan types is another trait, and a nearly unique one, linking Langton Bay with Thule material at Booth Island.

The large whaling harpoon head from Okat substantiates ethnographic evidence of bowhead whale hunting in Franklin Bay. It must have been similar to the open-water whaling practiced by Mackenzie Inuit at Pt. Atkinson and Cape Bathurst (see Morrison

IGLULUALUMIUT PREHISTORY

1988a: 91-97), where nearly identical whaling heads have also been discovered (Wissler 1916: 418; Mathiassen 1930: 8). Alaskan whaling harpoon heads are also of the same form (Stanford 1976: 23).

Both the Thule and Recent occupations share similar fixed antler lance heads. They are very similar to Eastern Thule specimens, especially those from the Silumiut site on the northwestern coast of Hudson Bay (McCartney 1977: Pl 7), and quite unlike usual Western Arctic styles (see Murdoch 1892: 240; Ford 1959: 105). A somewhat similar but larger lance head is reported from the historic Mackenzie Inuit Kugaluk site (Morrison 1988a: 40).

Also common to most of the Franklin Bay sites are long, barbed dart heads. Specimens from Iglulualuit and Booth Island are particularly similar, and closely resemble a dart head from Barter Island (Mathiassen 1930: Pl 5, fig. 6). Generally similar dart heads, however, are very widespread.

Other weapons used in sea mammal hunting are widely distributed. The throwing harpoon used in boat or ice-edge hunting is well attested by the solid Class 1 socketpieces found at Langton Bay and Okat, and perhaps also by the much lighter, tubular socketpieces from Iglulualuit and Booth Island. Both of these socket forms are widespread Eskimo types. The comparatively short, straight loose foreshafts from Booth Island would also be very well adapted to a throwing harpoon. They are very similar to foreshafts from other western Canadian Arctic Thule sites (Morrison 1983a: Pl. 7), and can be distinguished from the longer, more curved foreshafts from the Recent Franklin Bay sites. These latter closely resemble foreshafts from the Mackenzie Inuit (Wissler 1916: Fig. 38,g; Mathiassen 1930: 8; Morrison 1988a: 39), and might be associated with breathing-hole sealing. Both Langton Bay and Okat also produced short, fixed foreshafts, like those from Eastern Thule (Mathiassen 1927a: Pl. 3, fig. 5) or Kotzebue

CHAPTER 3: SEA MAMMAL HUNTING GEAR

culture (Giddings and Anderson 1986: Pl. 1, d-e).

Aside from foreshafts, clear evidence of breathing-hole sealing during the Recent period comes from Langton Bay, in the form of a sealing stool. A probable seal indicator from Booth Island suggests that sophisticated breathing-hole sealing techniques may have been already developed by Thule times, if however it is identified correctly and is not intrusive (see Morrison 1983b). It is the only seal indicator to be identified from a Thule context anywhere in Arctic North America. Ice hunting gear also includes wound pins, found only at Booth Island, and ubiquitous drag handles.

It can be noted that the seal netting described ethnographically for the Iglulualuit site has no reflection in the recovered artifacts from any of the Franklin Bay sites.

Chapter 4
LAND HUNTING GEAR
Iglulualuit

Arrowheads

Most of the twelve bone or antler arrowheads appear to be variants on a common theme (Pl. 8, i-n). Eight are complete at the proximal end, and of these seven have comparatively slight but squared shoulders and a sharp conical tang. On one example this tang is plain; the others exhibit two sharp spurs to make the attachment to a wooden shaft more secure. The seventh specimen has evidently been re-worked from a similar configuration to a split-based form, presumably as the result of a break (Pl. 8, m).

Barbing tends to be unilateral, with only one bilaterally barbed specimen. Four exhibit multi-barbing. Barb position varies widely, from below the mid-point to very close to the tip, and from comparatively small to very large. Only four specimens exhibit incised "guide lines" delineating the barb area. Three specimens exhibit a socket cut in the distal end for the accommodation of an endblade (Pl. 8, k-m). Sockets lack rivet holes, and are comparatively wide (about 5 mm), and are gouged rather than cut. Each was found with a suitable chipped-stone endblade within a few centimeters of the distal end (i.e. Pl. 8, f-h). They had evidently been secured by friction, perhaps aided by glue. Two of these endbladed arrowheads are made of whale bone, but all other arrowheads are antler. Lengths range from 88 to 247 mm.

An aberrant specimen is made of bone (Pl. 9, b). It resembles spear heads found at the site (see below), but is so small it presumably functioned on the end of an arrow. It has a serrated, wedge-shaped base, and a comparatively long, parallel-sided blade element, with a sharp-sided lenticular cross-section and neither barbs nor blade slots. The length is 50 mm.

CHAPTER 4: LAND HUNTING GEAR

Arrow Points

Chipped stone endblades small enough to have functioned as arrow points were fairly numerous. The function seems clear in the case of at least three, since they were found in close association with three arrowheads having endblade sockets. These three are all of a roughly tear-dropped shape, as are six other examples (Pl. 8, a-b, f-h). The collection also includes a few irregular lanceolates (Pl. 8, d), and points with slight, rounded shoulders and contracting stems (Pl. 8, e). There is also a bipoint (Pl. 8, c). All are made of quartzite, chert, or a coarser-grained basaltic material. Lengths range from 28 to 49 mm.

Archery Gear

Blunt arrowheads or **bunts** for bird hunting are made of antler or whale bone (Pl. 9, e-g). Of five specimens, one is unfinished, while the other four show a range of tang forms. Two have split bases with recessed lashing beds, one has a wedge-shaped tang with slight lateral knobs, and one has a simple drilled socket. Three have tri-lobate tips, one a four-lobed tip, and one a simple, blunt end. A broken **sinew twister** and a **marlin spike** (Pl. 9, a) are made of antler, while a second marlin spike is made of whale bone. Both tools were used in the manipulation of the sinew backing of traditional Eskimo bows. The nock end of a **bow** was also recovered. An antler **archer's wrist guard** is plain, with a pair of connected holes near either edge to hold a lashing (Pl. 8, o).

Spear Points

The distal portion of a large chipped stone endblade exhibits rounded lateral margins, a fairly blunt tip, no real shoulders, and an apparently straight-sided stem (Pl. 9, h). The extant length is 70 mm, by 46 mm wide. Other specimens are

IGLULUALUMIUT PREHISTORY

smaller, but still too large to have functioned as arrow points. Two are bipointed, one with a narrow, contracting stem (Pl. 9, i), and the other with a distinct point-of-juncture on either lateral margin. A fourth specimen has a lanceolate outline and a straight base (Pl. 9, j), while a fifth, also with a straight base, has well-marked shoulders and a rectangular stem (Pl. 9, k). There is also an unfinished specimen, and a tip fragment. Specimens are made of dark or brown chert, or quartzite, and range from 58 to 66 mm long. They resemble the points of bear or deer lances used by historic north Alaskan people (Murdoch 1892: 242).

Two other large points are made of non-siliceous material, and share a common outline (Pl. 9, c-d). One is made of bone, and the other of ground slate. They have a long, leaf-shaped blade section, slight shoulders, a long, serrated stem, and a rounded base. The aberrant arrowhead described above is of the same shape. Lengths are 94.5 and 104 mm, respectively.

Langton Bay

Arrowheads

Of twenty-five arrowheads from Langton Bay, 18 are complete at the proximal end, and represent several types not found at Iglulualuit (Pl. 10, Pl. 11, a-b). The most common tang formation, however, is the same; a spurred, conical tang set below well-marked, squared shoulders. Next most common is a plain conical tang, in one case set below a squared shoulder, but in three others associated with only a weak, sloping shoulder, or none at all. Two arrowheads have "knobbed" tangs, one has a "conically-knobbed" tang, two have "ringed" tangs (see Morrison 1983a: 112-117, 177 for definitions), while one specimen has a wedge-shaped base and a final specimen has a deep socket gouged in the proximal end. Other features do not appear to be related to tang form. Four specimens are made of whale bone and 21 of antler. Barbing is usually unilateral and often single,

CHAPTER 4: LAND HUNTING GEAR

with only two examples showing a pair of opposite barbs. Six specimens have provision for an endblade. In three cases this is a simple distal slit, flanked by one or a pair of cut barbs. Three others have a gouged slot, like the endblade slots appearing on Iglulualuit arrowheads. None shows any decoration beyond the occasional barb line. Two specimens, however, have a tiny raised point or nipple on a barb edge, similar to the raised points described on harpoon heads. Lengths range from 110 to 171 mm.

Archery Gear

Three antler **bird bunts** take a similar form (Pl. 11, f-i). All have smooth, un-lobed faces, and split bases with shallow lashing beds. A fourth specimen is again unlobed, but has a wedge-shaped base, with slight notches or projections on the side. Lengths range from 67.5 to 74 mm. A flat antler rectangle (29.5 x 23 x 2.5 mm) with concave margins (Pl. 11, e) is similar to specimens from western Alaska described as gaming pieces (Giddings 1952: 91). McGhee (1974: 53), following Jenness (1946: 124), identifies them as **wedges for tightening the sinew backing of bows**. Two bird bone shafts have been cut obliquely at the end to form a sharp, spatulate tip (Pl. 11, c-d). They resemble **arrow featherers** described by Jenness (1946: 131).

Dagger

A dagger has been manufactured from the leg bone of a large animal, probably a bear ulna (Pl. 11, j). It comes to a point, and the slightly curving lateral margins have been ground sharp. There is a suspension hole at the proximal end, below which can be seen the faint lines left by a sinew or hide wrapping around the handle. It is 261 mm long. Among Mackenzie Inuit, polar bear-bone daggers were a favourite fighting weapon in early historic times (Stefansson 1914a: 187).

IGLULUALUMIUT PREHISTORY

Okat

Arrowheads

Of six antler arrowheads, only four are intact at the proximal end (Pl. 12, a-d). All have squared shoulders and conical tangs; in three cases these tangs are further equipped with a pair of small spurs. All specimens are unilaterally barbed, and most have guide lines incised along the inside of the barb. The only other apparent attempt at decoration is a small spur on a barb edge, similar to that exhibited by one of the Langton Bay arrowheads. Another arrowhead has a narrow endblade slit.

Arrow Points

Nine chert arrow points probably represent the same "type," with square to rounded shoulders, a rectangular tang, and a triangular blade element (Pl. 12, e-m). Lengths range from 29 to 45 mm.

Archery Gear

A fragmentary **bird bunt** has an unlobed, bluntly conical distal end. A wooden **sinew twister** is of typical form and 93 mm long (Pl. 12, n). Two arrow **shaft straighteners** are made on heavy antler sections with a large ovate hold gouged in one end (Pl. 12, o).

Booth Island

Arrowheads

Nineteen bone and antler arrowheads include 11 which are intact at the proximal end (Pl. 13, a-j). Four tang forms are represented, all similar to forms at Langton Bay, Okat, and Iglulualuit, but in different frequencies. Most common is the ringed tang, represented by five specimens; followed by the

CHAPTER 4: LAND HUNTING GEAR

familiar spurred tang, of which there are four examples. Conically knobbed and knobbed tangs are both represented by single examples. In most cases, shoulders are as square as those on arrowheads from Iglulualuit, Langton Bay and Okat, but there are several exceptions with the sloping shoulders more characteristic of earlier Thule sites in the Western Arctic (see Stanford 1976: 33-36). As elsewhere, barbing varies widely, but there is a tendency for it to be unilateral. There is no evidence of endblading, or of ownership marks, while decoration is restricted to incised lines running along the interior edge of barbs, and a single Y-motif. One specimen has a sharp raised point or nipple below the barbing on one edge, similar to the raised points on some of the arrowheads from Okat and Langton Bay. Lengths range from 88.5 mm to 185 mm.

Arrow Points

Two small quartzite endblades have triangular blade sections and long, contracting stems, set below rounded shoulders (Pl. 13, k-l). The complete example is 48.5 mm long.

Archery Gear

A single whale bone **bird bunt** again has a smooth, unlobed face, and a socketed base to accommodate the arrow shaft. A complete **sinew twister** for a bow is 97 mm long and made of whale bone.

Discussion

Arrowhead tang forms appear to be time-sensitive, but show little obvious regional variation, at least within the broad limits of Western Eskimo culture. In the Kobuk River sequence, specimens with square shoulders and spurred tangs like those found on a majority of specimens from Iglulualuit, Okat and Langton Bay are particularly characteristic of the 18th century Ambler Island

IGLULUALUMIUT PREHISTORY

TABLE 3

Location of Land Hunting Gear: Franklin Bay Sites

	Iglulualuit H 11	H 20	Misc.	Langton	Okat	Booth
Arrowheads: spurred tang	1	4	1	7	3	4
plain tang		1		4	1	
socketed base		1		1		
wedge tang		1		1		
knobbed tang				2		1
ringed tang				2		5
c.-knobbed tang				1		1
distal fragments		3		7	2	8
Arrow points: tear-drop	3	6				
bipoint		1				
contracting stem	1	1				2
irreg. lanceolate	1	1				
rectangular stem					9	
fragment		1				
Bird bunts	4	1			1	1
Bow	1					
Bow wedge				1		
Arrow featherer				2		
Sinew twister	1				1	1
Marlin spikes	1	1				
Wrist guard	1					
Arrow straightener					2	
Spear points: chipped stone	2	5				
ground stone		1				
bone		1				
Dagger				1		

---

site (Giddings 1952: 43). They are similarly characteristic of the Kotzebue culture arrowheads at Cape Krusenstern (Giddings and Anderson 1986: 48), and Recent arrowheads at Pt. Barrow (Ford 1959: Fig. 63; Stanford 1976:43). Among Mackenzie Inuit sites, spurred tangs are found at the historic Kugaluk (Morrison 1988a: 41), Barry (Morrison 1988b) and Bombadier Channel sites (Arnold 1986), and are characteristic of the post-A.D. 1600 levels at Kittigazuit (McGhee 1974: Table 2). "Ringed," "knobbed" and

CHAPTER 4: LAND HUNTING GEAR

"conically-knobbed" tangs are generally earlier. The former is most common at Booth Island, and is also particularly characteristic of arrowheads from Ekseavik or Late Western Thule in the west Alaskan sequence (A.D. 1300 to 1400; Giddings 1952: 45; Giddings and Anderson 1986: 62). Knobbed tangs, again present at Booth Island, are most characteristic of the following Intermediate Kotzebue phase (A.D. 1550; Giddings 1952: 43), and also occur in the lower levels at Kittigazuit (McGhee 1974: Table 2), and at the early Mackenzie Inuit site of Radio Creek (McGhee 1974: 78). These earlier types also occur at Langton Bay, although they are less common than the spurred tang. This observation corroborates the mixed or transitional status of that site, as suggested on the basis of the harpoon heads.

Endblade slots of any sort are comparatively unusual on late prehistoric arrowheads; the gouged form of the Iglulualuit and Langton Bay slots is similar to those on arrowheads from Radio Creek (McGhee 1974: 78), and also from the Kobuk River (Giddings 1952: 50).

Chipped-stone arrow points are in themselves a Western Eskimo trait, but at the same time show an interesting range of variation. Iglulualuit arrow points are predominantly tear-dropped shaped, and lack the well-defined rectangular stem present on all of the Okat specimens. The Iglulualuit arrowheads are the more unusual, but can nonetheless be matched at Kittigazuit, where they seem to be primarily associated with the lower, pre-A.D. 1600 levels (McGhee 1974: 50-51). Similar points also appear at Pt. Atkinson (N1Tk-2; ASC collections), and in the earlier sites of the Kobuk River sequence (Giddings 1952: 50). Rectangular or square-stemmed arrowheads seem to be particularly associated with very late sites prehistoric sites in Alaska, and the post-A.D. 1600 levels at Kittigazuit (Giddings 1952: Fig. 26-27; Ford 1959: Table 1; Stanford 1976: 37; McGhee 1974: 50). Okat may thus be more recent than Iglulualuit. The absence of arrow points from

IGLULUALUMIUT PREHISTORY

Langton Bay is unfortunate, but presumably due to happenstance.

The Booth Island arrow points also lack well-defined stems. They loosely resemble "knife blades" found at Nunagiak (Ford 1959: Fig. 82), and bipointed and contracting-stem points from Ekseavik (Giddings 1952: Pl. XXVIII) and Iglulualuit. A closer comparison, however, can be made with arrow points from the Jackson site at Cape Parry (Taylor 1972: Pl. 2,i), and Clachan, where similar points were originally but probably mistakenly attributed to a small Palaeoeskimo component there (Morrison 1983a: Pl. 35, a-b).

The large chipped-stone spear points from Iglulualuit provide another link between that site and Kittigazuit (McGhee 1974: 52), and also west Alaska (Giddings 1952: 51). Although similar points were used by historic north Alaskans (Murdoch 1892: 242), their apparent absence from prehistoric contexts there suggests to McGhee (1974: 89) that they are a specific Mackenzie Inuit-west Alaskan "type."

Other items of terrestrial-hunting gear are mostly of types and styles common to most Eskimo cultures of the last thousand years. Included are a bow fragment, wrist guard, marlin spikes, arrow featherers, shaft straighteners, sinew twisters, and the large bone dagger from Langton Bay. One possibly distinctive local trait is the smooth, flat or bluntly conical face of the antler and whale bone bird bunts from both Thule and Recent sites. In most other areas these are usually facetted or lobed. It may be significant that bird bunts from the Clachan site on western Coronation Gulf, and from Kittigazuit, are also sometimes smooth-faced (Morrison 1983a: 118; McGhee 1974: 50). Tang form is typical of most Arctic sites.

Chapter 5
Fishing Gear
Iglulualuit

Fish Hooks

Two styles of fish hook-shank are represented at Iglulualuit:

<u>Class 1</u>: A very large specimen consists of a long (111.5 mm), narrow (10.5 mm) bar of antler, with a sub-rectangular cross-section, and tapered slightly toward the proximal end, where it is equipped with two drilled suspension holes (Pl. 14, a). The distal end has a larger hole for the barb, which is missing. Five narrow holes have been drilled from side to side through the width of the piece, some of them still holding copper plugs. They may have functioned as weights as well as ornaments. A second, apparently smaller specimen is broken (Pl. 14, b).

<u>Class 2</u>: These shanks are much smaller (23-32 mm long), with a rounded, tear-drop outline. There are two specimens (Pl. 14, c-d), and again, each has a drilled hole on each lateral margin to take a plug or inlay. One still has a copper barb and one extant copper inlay.

A single **loose barb** is made of bone, and is too large to fit any of the recovered shanks (Pl. 14, e). It is 58 mm long, curved, and tapers to a sharp point. The proximal end is pierced by a rivet hole, within which is a broken bone rivet.

Leister Prongs

Seven barbed bone and antler prongs and one wooden prong appear to represent both fish spears and arrows. Four are comparatively large (135 to 162 mm long), and probably represent spear prongs (Pl. 14, g-h; Pl. 36, d). Two of them have conical bases indicating end hafting, while the other two have a base with a triangular cross-section and an outside lashing knob, indicating side hafting. The shape and number of barbs varies considerably, but is invariably unilateral. The four smaller arrow prongs are

IGLULUALUMIUT PREHISTORY

83 to 103 mm long, and much more delicate (Pl. 14, f, i-k). Again barbing is unilateral. All appear to have been end-hafted.

Ice Picks

Only very rough ice picks were recovered, consisting of trimmed and pointed antler beam sections 154 to 170 mm long. The tips are polished and usually shows some wear, while the proximal ends are cut square and roughened on both faces. Cross-sections are uniformly plano-convex, reflecting manufacture on split antler tines. Most are thick enough they could only have been hafted in a heavy, open socket. They may have been used in fishing or, possibly, hafted to the butt end of an ice-hunting harpoon.

Langton Bay

Fish Hooks

Fish hook shanks are well represented in the Langton Bay collection, which includes several classes not represented at Iglulualuit. Long, narrow Class 1 fish hook shanks with drilled lateral holes to take inlays are represented by three specimens, two made of antler and one of whale bone (Pl. 15, a-c). Two are complete, or nearly so, and have lengths of 62 to 65 mm. Two Class 2 "tom cod" shanks are both flat and tear-drop shaped, without lateral inlay holes, and are made of bone or ivory (Pl. 15, d-e). As well as the barb and suspension hole, both have a pattern of small holes drilled through the face. Lengths are 34.5 and 37 mm. Two new formal classes can be defined:

<u>Class 3</u>: Plain, simple shanks, with elongated outlines, ovate cross-sections, and no inlay holes. The three examples have a large barb hole at one end, and a small drilled suspension hole at the other (Pl. 15, f-h). Two are made of antler, and one of whale bone, and lengths average about 65 mm.

<u>Class 4</u>: Short, heavy antler shanks, with an ovate outline, and a thick, plano-convex cross-section. Two specimens are 40 and 43 mm

CHAPTER 5: FISHING GEAR

long, and have one to two suspension holes and a large hole for the hook (Pl. 15, i-j).

Five **loose barbs** are made of bone, and have lengths of 50 to 65 mm (Pl. 15, k-o). They are slightly less curved than the Iglulualuit specimen, and most have notches at the base to hold them in place in the shank. They are rather subjectively distinguished from the trident barbs described below on the basis of their smaller size, and the presence of these notches.

Lures

A single fish-shaped lure is made of antler, with a mid-line skeletal motif, a drilled eye-hole, and three drilled suspension holes (Pl. 15, z). The tail is missing, but the original length would have been about 56 mm. A much different lure is shaped like a modern fishing spoon (Pl. 15, aa). It has a drilled suspension hole, is made of whale bone, and is 58 mm long.

Leister Prongs

A barbed antler side prong 128.5 mm long is possibly from a fish spear (Pl. 15, t). Unlike Iglulualuit specimens it is bilaterally barbed, but has the same tang form, with a triangular cross-section and a notched and roughed back to hold the binding. Two other broken specimens are unilaterally barbed (Pl. 15, s). There are also two small fish arrow prongs 82 and 90 mm long, again with unilateral barbing (Pl. 15, q-r). One appears to have been side mounted, and the other end hafted.

Trident or Three-Pronged Fish Spear

Five large bone barbs can be tentatively distinguished as trident barbs (Pl. 15, u-y). They are between 67 and 89 mm long, straight to slightly curved in outline, with a pointed distal end and a blunt proximal end. Without lashing holes, they would have been inserted through the side prongs of the three-pronged fishing

IGLULUALUMIUT PREHISTORY

trident. What may be a centre prong for a similar type of fish spear is made of antler, and 161.5 mm long (Pl. 15, p). It comes to a sharp point distally, while the other end has been carefully thinned to form a wedge-shaped base equipped with a lashing hole.

Ice Picks

A large antler ice pick is very well made, with straight lateral margins, slight shoulders, and a wedge-shaped, slightly roughed haft (Pl. 15, bb). It is 285 mm long. Three other picks are shorter (150-180 mm long), much more roughly-made, and similar to examples from Iglulualuit.

Okat

Leister Prongs

The few leister prongs are all of the large, spear size (Pl. 16, a-d). A complete specimen is 160 mm long, bilaterally barbed and tanged for side hafting. A unilaterally barbed specimen is of similar size, but unfinished. Also in the collection is a broken centre prong, and the tip of a centre or side prong. All are made of antler.

Ice Scoops

Two specimens made from wide sections of antler cortex are split distally, with paired holes which would have held a netting (Pl. 16, e-f). Both are broken, so that the form of the handle cannot be determined.

Ice Picks

Rough split-antler ice picks are particularly abundant in the Okat collection. There are 39 complete specimens, similar to those already described from Iglulualuit. Lengths range from 134 to about 210 mm (Pl. 16, j-k).

CHAPTER 5: FISHING GEAR

Booth Island

Fish Hooks

Three fish hook shanks are all made of whale bone, and have a similar, slightly curved fish-like shape (Pl. 16, l-n). The proximal end is represented by a narrow tail, unfortunately broken in all three cases, so it cannot be determined if specimens were equipped with a suspension groove or hole. One has a secondary suspension hole through the "back." A connected pair of drilled holes at the distal end would have held the hook, which must have been of metal. Two of the three are drilled through just above the distal end to accommodate a plug inlay, again presumably of copper. Otherwise, there is no decoration. Cross-sections are ovate to sub-triangular, and complete lengths are estimated at about 85 to 90 mm.

Lures

Fish-shaped lures differ from hook shanks in that they were suspended dorsally rather than from the tail, and of course in lacking provision for barb attachment (Pl. 16, g-i). One very large specimen has a round cross-section, drilled eyes (which presumably held inlays), and three slotted suspension holes. The mouth is indicated by an incised line, a deep incision encircles the neck, while a vertebral motif runs through the mid-line. It is 142 mm long, and made of whale bone. A much smaller antler specimen (extant length: 58 mm) has drilled suspension holes, and again a vertebral motif. The tail is missing. A third specimen is badly damaged, but apparently plain. Similar lures are common to most Inuit sites.

Leister Prongs

As at other sites, there is a dichotomy in size among barbed whale bone and antler leister prongs. Seven are of a size suggestive of fish arrow prongs, with lengths between 78 and about

IGLULUALUMIUT PREHISTORY

120 mm. Tang form ranges from conical to spatulate, but only one specimen is asymmetrical enough to suggest side hafting. It is also the only specimen with unilateral barbing.

A very much larger side prong is made of whale bone, with a triangular butt indicative of side hafting, and a row of five barbs cut along the inside edge. It is 185 mm long, and much more heavily constructed than the presumed arrow prongs. A second example is rather unusual. It has a pair of opposite barbs and is made of antler, with a concave/convex cross-section. It was apparently hafted by being lashed to a shaft placed against the concave face. Evidence of the lashing is still visible, and there is a hole to accommodate the end of the lashing near the butt. The broken tip of a third large, bilaterally barbed antler specimen is also represented.

Trident or Three-Pronged Fish Spear

A thick antler barb 65 mm long has three drilled lashing holes. It represents the common Thule type of trident barb.

Ice Picks

Two slender antler ice picks have pointed, roughened tang elements and lengths of 148 and 209 mm. Other examples are more rough and have square-cut butts.

Discussion

Probably the most important aspect of the fishing gear from Franklin Bay is a negative one; the absence of netting equipment. This has been commented on by Stefansson (1913: 332; 1914a: 332), and supported by his ethnographic informants. Panigyuk, the woman born near Langton Bay in the 1830s, never saw fish nets in her own community, although she had heard of their use to the west. Even at Baillie Island they were said to have been adopted only recently. The absence of fish nets in Franklin Bay is

CHAPTER 5: FISHING GEAR

TABLE 4

Location of Fishing Gear: Franklin Bay Sites

	Iglulualuit H 11	H 20	Misc.	Langton	Okat	Booth
Fish hook shanks:						
Class 1	1	1		3		
Class 2	1	1		2		
Class 3				3		
Class 4				2		
fish-shaped						3
Hooks, bone	1			5		
Lures, fish-shaped				1		3
other				1		
Leister prongs, large	2	3		3	4	3
small	1	2		2		7
Trident barb, pin type				5		
Thule type						1
Trident centre prong				1		
Ice scoop					2	
Ice picks	1	2	1	4	39	4

----

curious considering ethnographic statements about the use of sealnets at Iglulualuit (Stefansson 1914a: 352). A bone net gauge from a historic site at Whale Cove, between Iglulualuit and Baillie Island (American Museum of Natural History collections: 60.1-3258) is probably the most easterly fish-netting item known, except for a few very tentatively identified net fragments from Eastern Thule contexts (Mathiassen 1927b: 58). Netting gear occurs commonly in Mackenzie Inuit and west Alaskan sites, and seems to distinguish Thule from Recent assemblages in at least the western part of the Mackenzie Inuit area (McGhee 1974: 79; Yorga 1980: 84).

    Western style fish-hook shanks from Iglulualuit and Langton Bay loosely resemble specimens from the west Alaskan sequence (Giddings 1952: 40), but are unlike the stick-like types most

IGLULUALUMIUT PREHISTORY

characteristic of the more recent assemblages (Giddings 1952: 36-38). They are more like those found in Mackenzie Inuit sites, where the Class 2 specimens resemble what McGhee (1974: 55) calls tomcod shanks (see also Mathiassen 1930: Pl. 1, fig. 10-11). Class 3 specimens are also similar to shanks from Kittigazuit (McGhee's 1974: 54), Pt. Atkinson (Mathiassen 1930: Pl. 1, fig. 8). Class 4 shanks, by contrast, resemble the bone or antler setting used to secure a fish hook by historic Copper Inuit (Jenness 1946: Fig. 128), and are unlike other Western Arctic specimens. Fish hooks were apparently not used in north Alaska until historic times (Ford 1959: 150), and are rare to absent in Eastern Thule (Mathiassen 1927b: 57).

Comparatively large fish-shaped shanks like those from Booth Island seem to compare best with specimens from Ekseavik in west Alaska (Giddings 1952: 38). Similarities with Class 1 and 3 shanks seem more general. Fish-hook shanks first appear in the western Alaskan sequence during late Thule times, ie. between about A.D. 1300 and 1400, so that the Ekseavik specimens are among the earliest (Giddings and Anderson 1986: 63). Western-style fish-hook shanks also appear in late Thule contexts at the Washout site on Herschel Island (Yorga 1980: 79), the Jackson site at Cape Parry (Taylor 1972: 18), and from an unpublished Thule site at the mouth of the Inman River, between Cape Parry and Coronation Gulf (ASC collections; illustrated in Jenness 1922: Fig. 10).

Isolated bone hooks from Iglulualuit and Langton Bay can be exactly matched by specimens from Kittigazuit (McGhee 1974: 55), Ekseavik, and Intermediate Kotzebue (Giddings 1952: Pl. 29, fig. 16; Pl. 36, fig. 12-14). Absent, however, are the straight, notched hooks common to most Mackenzie Inuit sites (see Morrison 1988a: 44).

Spearing equipment is well represented. Most sites include both large and small barbed side and centre-prongs, which would have been used with spears and fish arrows, respectively. This

CHAPTER 5: FISHING GEAR

apparent use of fish arrows suggests a connection with Mackenzie Inuit and West Alaskan Inupiat (see McGhee 1974: 56; Giddings 1952: 37-38; Giddings 1964: 47). The three-pronged trident fish spear is represented by separate barbs for the side prongs from Langton Bay and Booth Island. It may be significant that the single Booth Island specimens is of the usual Thule style, with lashing holes, while the Recent examples are of the simple pin type (see Mathiassen 1927b: 55; Giddings 1952: 36; Ford 1959: 149).

Fish-shaped lures, split-bowl ice scoops, and split antler ice picks are also present at most sites. All of these are of common Eskimo types.

CHAPTER 6
TRANSPORTATION GEAR
Iglulualuit

Sledding Gear

Of five broken **sled shoes**, one is antler and four of whalebone. Widths range from 18 to 30 mm, and all have drilled peg holes (Pl. 18, f, h).

Miscellaneous

Two nearly identical whale bone shafts are 8.5 to 9 mm in diametre and 157 to 188 mm long (Pl. 18, i). One end has been cut aslant and roughened for lashing, while the opposite end comes to a blunt, strongly shouldered point. They appear to represent the handle ends of **snow probes**. Additional sections would have been attached from the scarfed end, to form an implement perhaps 1.5 m long.

Three eyed needles are tentatively identified as **snow shoe needles** (Pl. 18, g). Two are complete, and are 85 and 123 mm long, respectively, with ovate cross-sections achieving a maximum diametre of about 7 mm. The distal end comes to a sharp point, while a narrow line hole has been drilled about 20 mm above the proximal end. The longer example is made of bone; the shorter and a broken example are made of antler. Snow shoe parts appear at Kittigazuit (McGhee 1974: 59), and somewhat similar needles occur in the later stages of the Kobuk River sequence (Giddings 1952: 61).

Langton Bay

Sledding Gear

Five **sled shoe** fragments are all made of whale bone, with drilled holes and widths of 25 to 28 mm (Pl. 20, d).

Miscellaneous

What appears to be the broken, handle end of a **snow probe** has a round cross-section, a distinct shoulder, and a conical

CHAPTER 6: TRANSPORTATION GEAR

proximal end, or tang (Pl. 20, g), around which a separate handle would fit.

Okat

Sledding Gear

What appears to be one end of a bone **swivel pin** for a dog harness was recovered (Pl. 23, e). Typical whale bone and antler **sled shoes** were also quite abundant (Pl. 23, d).

Miscellaneous

Of four **snow probe** fragments, three are shafts 200 to 300 mm long, with at least one end scarfed for attachment, and diameters of about 9 mm. The fourth shaft seems to represent the handle end, for it expands abruptly at one end, which is pierced for suspension (Pl. 23, a).

Booth Island

Sledding Gear

Sledding gear was again restricted to **sled shoe** fragments (Pl. 27, f-g). Five have drilled holes and widths ranging from 27 to 32.5 mm.

Miscellaneous

Snow probes were extremely abundant at Booth Island, with at least 38 individual specimens, representing a minimum of 14 complete probes. Each was apparently made by lashing together several lengths of whalebone shaft, each of which has been cut aslant at one or both ends, and averaging about 9 mm in diameter. Eight specimens represent the distal end, which swells into a pointed, egg-shaped form, and comes in varying lengths (Pl. 27, c-d, h-i). Four are unbroken, and have lengths ranging from 63 to 215 mm. There are 16 apparent mid-sections, only one of which is complete, with scarfing at either end. It is 221 mm long, but

IGLULUALUMIUT PREHISTORY

TABLE 5
Location of Transportation Gear: Franklin Bay

	Iglulualuit H 11	H 20	Misc.	Langton	Okat	Booth
Swivel pin					1	
Sled shoes	2	1	2	5	26	5
Snow probe pieces	1		1	1	4	38
Snoe shoe needles?		2	1			

---

several of the broken specimens are longer. Probable proximal ends come in two styles. The most common, represented by 12 specimens, has an expanded end, with a rough trianguloid or sub-rectangular cross-section, about 12 mm thick, and often with a gouged or drilled suspension hole (Pl. 27, e). The other style, with two examples, is like that described for Iglulualuit, wherein a blunt, shouldered tang is provided to the attachment of a separate handle.

Discussion

As is usual in Western Arctic sites, evidence of sledding is limited in most of the Franklin Bay sites to actual sled parts, with little direct evidence of dog traction. All four sites produced whale bone sled shoe fragments, with drilled peg holes and widths of about 25 mm. None is long enough to give any idea of the type of sled to which they were attached. A very short komatik style of sled was usual in the Mackenzie Inuit area (see McGhee 1974: 59), and a "runner of western type" from such a sled was found but apparently not collected by Stefansson at Langton Bay (Stefansson 1914a: 312). The only other item of sledding gear was a broken swivel pin from a dog harness, recovered from Okat. It is similar to specimens from the Mackenzie Inuit Kugaluk site (Morrison 1988a: 45), and to rare specimens from western Alaska

CHAPTER 6: TRANSPORTATION GEAR

(Giddings 1952: 59). Such pins are more characteristic of the Eastern and Central Arctic (see Jenness 1946: Fig. 178).

Whale bone rods from snow probes were strangely abundant, especially at Booth Island. They are primarily found in the Eastern and Central Arctic (Mathiassen 1927b: 67; Morrison 1983a: 135), but do occur at Kittigazuit in the Mackenzie Delta area (McGhee 1974: 65). Alaskan specimens are rare and appear to have been made exclusively of wood, with only a ferrule of antler or whale bone (Ford 1959: 142; Stanford 1976: 39).

CHAPTER 7
MEN'S TOOLS
Iglulualuit

Knives and Gravers

Two antler pieces rivetted together represent the proximal end of an **endbladed knife handle** (Pl. 17, b). One piece includes the actual blade socket, below which it has been split laterally to form a V-shaped concavity, into which fits the second piece. They are joined by five bone rivets. A butt section similar to the proximal socket piece would be needed to complete the handle. The socket is sufficiently narrow (20 x 2.5 mm) it presumably held a metal blade, although there is no evidence of rust staining. The unilaterally expanded butt of a second, whalebone, knife handle was also found (Pl. 17,d).

A short (94 mm) one-piece antler handle has a drilled suspension hole near one end and an endblade slit at the other (Pl. 17, a). It thus resembles the more usual type of simple, end-bladed flensing knife. What is unusual is the presence of a fox incisor wedged in a perfectly-fitting gouged hole near the blade end. This incisor shows grinding and polishing on a small facet at the tip, indicating use as a **graver**. Three similarly facetted fox incisors were also found, without associated handles. A second graving tool or burin again has a short antler handle (59 mm long), with a drilled suspension hole and an endblade socket (Pl. 17, c). Within it is a flat copper blade, held in place by two copper rivets. Two other graving tool handles are made of wood, and take a pencil-like shape about 110 mm long (Pl. 36, e-f). One has a tiny blade socket in one end, while the other has a similar socket at both ends. The bits, which are not present, would have been secured with a lashing, and may have been of iron.

Knife endblades can be divided into at least three morphological classes. All are made of ground slate, generally of a grey/black colour in the case of smaller specimens, and greenish

CHAPTER 7: MEN'S TOOLS

in the case of larger ones. The sample is too small to determine if this distinction is accidental, or the result of the deliberate choice of different lithic types for different functions. Several sawn slate fragments (Pl. 18, c-d) suggest preliminary shaping using stone saws.

Large, double-edged: Most common are large, stemmed, symmetrical knife blades. One complete example is 120 mm long, with small but quite definite shoulders and a large, square stem (Pl. 17, j). The blade margins are slightly excurvate, and both have been ground sharp without edge facets. A broken specimen is more roughly made, with the preparatory chipping showing through incomplete edge grinding. It has rounded shoulders and a narrower stem. A third example is complete but unfinished, exhibiting only very limited grinding (Pl. 17, i). It too has a rectangular stem and rounded shoulders, and has a total length of 142.5 mm. A final distal fragment can provisionally be placed in this category.

Small, double-edged: A single complete knife blade is much smaller (57.5 mm long), but is again two-edged, with well-defined, nearly square shoulders (Pl. 17, m). It has a triangular blade section and a slightly rounded base. Six fragmentary specimens may have been similar (Pl. 17, n).

Irregular: A final complete endblade has a nearly symmetrical, leaf-shaped, double-edged blade section which has been fully ground without edge facetting (Pl. 17, k). It has been left unfinished where the tang or stem would be. Since it appears otherwise completed, it may simply have been hand-held without a handle. It is 116 mm long.

Other Manufacturing Tools

A short (96 mm) whalebone shaft comes to a strong, blunt point at one end, and may represent the point of a **flint flaker** (Pl. 17, e). The proximal end shows a wedge-shaped hafting element, indicating that it was used with a handle. A second antler specimen comes to a more spatulate end, which shows signs of heavy wear. It has been broken distally.

Five small socket-pieces may have functioned as **bit sockets for drills** (Pl. 17, f-h). They are from 39 to 51.5 mm long, with a rounded fore-end and a wedge-shaped tang. One example is made of ivory, and is better finished than the others, pierced by a drilled hole to hold a lashing. The other specimens are made of antler. Sockets are round to slightly ovate in plan, and about 10 mm deep. One socket is so small (ca. 1.5 x 1.5 mm) that it must have held a tiny metal bit. Other sockets vary between 3.5 x 3.5 mm and 3.5 x 6 mm, and probably held chipped stone or jade bits. An Ambler Island drill socket similar to these has been identified by Giddings (1952: Pl. IV, 12).

Two light wooden shafts functioned as **drill spindles** (Pl. 36, e-f). Both are about 210 mm long, with a large socket gouged in one end. They could not have been used with one of the bit sockets described above.

Of five **splitting wedges**, one is a large specimen made of whale bone 171 mm long, with a drilled hole near the butt end (Pl. 18, b). Four others are 67.5 to 89 mm long (Pl. 18, e). Three of them are made of antler, and one of whale bone.

Finally, a broken pebble has a polished facet on one face, suggesting use as a **whetstone**.

Mattocks

The abundance of large whale bone picks and mattocks at Iglulualuit is a reflection of the heavy clay into which the house pits had to be dug; a difficult enough task with metal shovels. Of twelve specimens, only three are more or less complete. They are 355 to 385 mm long and 80 to 110 mm wide, while the broken specimens include several which must have been significantly larger. All have a constricted, notched hafting element and a

CHAPTER 7: MEN'S TOOLS

broad, spatulate working end (Pl. 18, a). In most cases, the concave, lower face has been chopped flat for seating against a handle. At least four have a rounded cross-section suggestive of picks, while the others are broader and better classified as mattocks.

Langton Bay

Knives

The simple **endbladed knife handle** is well represented, consisting of a roughly-finished length of antler with a blade slot in one end and, usually, a suspension hole at the other (Pl. 19). Lengths range from 92 to more than 170 mm. Three have particularly small blade sockets (about 2.5 x 6 mm) with a rectangular cross-section, and must have been used with a tanged metal blade. Another specimen has a sideblade slit cut in each lateral margin.

Two large, well-finished knife handles are more elaborate. One has a blade slit rather than the more usual socket cut in the distal end (Pl. 19, e). There is no rivet hole, but the slit is sprung tight, so that the endblade would be held in place by pressure, aided by a lashing below the slight distal lip. Rather than a suspension hole, there is a groove cut around the proximal end. It is straight-sided, 210 mm long, and resembles historic Western Eskimo knives (Murdoch 1892: Fig. 99). The second handle is of the same length and material (antler). It has a slightly expanded distal end, a deep, rectangular-cut blade socket (4.5 x 16 mm), an expanded base, and raised square-cut hand grips on the lateral margins (Pl. 19, c). There is are two suspension holes, one drilled straight through and the other curved, exiting through the butt. There is also a drilled hole near the balance point. It closely resembles historic Copper Inuit knife handles (Jenness 1946: Fig. 107), especially an unpublished specimen found at the late prehistoric Copper Inuit site of Nadlok (see Gordon 1988).

IGLULUALUMIUT PREHISTORY

Two antler **sideblade knife handles** have blade slits cut in one lateral margin toward the distal end. Cross-sections take the ovate shape of the unmodified antler shaft, but are thinned and flattened at the blade end. One has an endblade socket at the other end, as already described, and is short (length: 94 mm) and comparatively straight (Pl. 19, a). The other is more curved, and has a suspension hole at the proximal end (Pl. 19, b). Both blade slits are about 23 mm long, and both were probably used with metal blades. Both also show evidence of having been produced by cutting through a closely-spaced line of small drilled holes.

Other Manufacturing Tools

Two antler **drill sockets** are 99 to 119.5 mm long; larger than the more tentatively identified specimens from Iglulualuit (Pl. 20, e-f). They have a round cross-section, and a round socket cut in the distal end to a depth of about 23 mm. This socket is open on one side, and provided with a recessed lashing bed. The other end terminates in a roughened wedge tang for attachment in a split-based shaft.

Antler and whale bone **wedges** vary from 89 to 182 mm long, with whale bone specimens tending to be larger (Pl. 20, b-c).

Snow Knife

The handle end of a single whale bone snow knife has a curved outline and a single shoulder on the concave face (Pl. 20, a). The curved handgrip terminates in a unilateral knob, again on the concave face, and is equipped with two drilled suspension holes. Four drilled holes on the outer margin probably secured a lashed grip.

Okat

Knives

Seven antler **endblade knife handles** are of the simple type,

CHAPTER 7: MEN'S TOOLS

although one has an incised ladder-decoration around the tip, and two others have blade slits in both ends (Pl. 21). Most of the sockets are very narrow, and would have taken metal blades. Lengths range from 74 to 165.5 mm. Five other handles have a more finished and elaborate outline, with bilaterally expanding proximal and/or distal ends. Two have square-cut hand grips in raised relief (Pl. 21, e-f); the heavier of the two, in particular, resembles the Copper Inuit-like specimen from Langton Bay. Another plain specimen is the distal element of a multi-part handle with a very wide distal end (Pl. 21, d). It has four drilled holes which might have held rivets for attachment to a lower, proximal piece, similar to a specimen from Pt. Atkinson (Mathiassen 1930: Pl. 2, fig. 7). All have rectangular, tapering blade sockets, clearly designed for thick, tanged, metal blades, and varying in size from 8 x 14 mm to 2.5 x 5 mm. Total lengths range from 145.5 to 201 mm. A final antler knife handle 144 mm long is comparatively broad, with a bilaterally expanded butt and a narrow blade slit, rather than a true socket (Pl. 21, a). There is a lashing bed around the outside to secure what may have been a slate blade. It resembles the "Western Eskimo" knife handle found at Langton Bay.

A large sideblade knife handle is like Langton Bay specimens (Pl. 21, k). It is 180 mm long, and consists of a simple antler shaft which has been thinned and flattened toward one end, where one of the lateral margins has been slit to make a blade socket, by cutting between a line of drilled holes. The socket is 23 mm long, and probably took a metal blade.

Adzes

Four whale bone adze heads represent a simplified version of the standard Thule form (Pl. 22, b-e). Butt ends are expanded slightly; distal to this the cross-section is nearly round, with a flattened dorsal surface for seating against the handle. Surfaces

IGLULUALUMIUT PREHISTORY

are very heavily roughened, to take a lashing. More forward still is the socket element, which has a larger, more ovate cross-section. Three of the four have a distinct shoulder separating the socket element from the rear hafting section. Sockets are closed and gouged, and apparently first roughed-out by drilling. Lengths range from 103 to 163 mm.

Other Manufacturing Tools

A **drill bit** is made of chipped chert (Pl. 23, f). It is 42.5 mm long and only 12.5 mm wide, with a comparatively long, rectangular stem and rounded shoulders. The cross-section is thick, and the tip shows crushing and polishing.

Seven **wedges** are all made of antler, and from 73.5 to 146 mm long.

A large **hammer** takes the form of a blunt, heavy section of whale bone 178 mm long. It is heavily pocked at one end (Pl. 23, b).

Mattocks

Six complete whale bone picks or mattocks are smaller than but otherwise similar to those from Iglulualuit (Pl. 22, a). They lack lashing holes, but have notched sides and a flat dorsal face for seating against a handle. Lengths range from about 220 to 320 mm. There are also two fragmentary specimens.

Snow Knife

A broken snow knife handle is like that described from Langton Bay (Pl. 23, c). It has a curved outline, a single shoulder on the inner, concave margin, and the hand-grip terminates in a unilateral knob, which is pierced for suspension. It is made of whale bone.

CHAPTER 7: MEN'S TOOLS

Booth Island

Knives and Gravers

Five **endblade knife handles** consist of simple antler shafts with a blade socket gouged in one end (Pl. 24, b-d). The three complete examples also have a drilled suspension hole in the butt end. At least three have blade slits narrow enough to suggest the use of narrow metal blades. Lengths range from 85 to 148 mm.

Composite knife handles consist of two antler or ivory halves lashed together around a tiny central blade slit. Murdoch (1892: 172) describes them as chisels. One such half was recovered from Booth Island; it is made of antler and is 93 mm long (Pl. 24, h). There is a ladder design roughly incised on one side. Two **gravers** take a simpler form, consisting of one-piece antler "pencils" with a metal bit inserted in one end (Pl. 24, i-j). One specimen has an empty socket, while the other is still equipped with a tiny iron point. Both are about 93 mm long.

Three slightly curving antler **sideblade knife handles** are very similar to specimens from Langton Bay (Pl. 24, e, g). All appear to have held metal blades, and in one case clear rust staining can be seen. The blade slits are 8 to 12 mm long, and overall handle lengths range from 151 to 170 mm. One specimen has a ladder-design incised on the end opposite the blade socket, two marginally-placed holes which may have held a knife-sharpener (cf. Jenness 1946: Fig. 114), and a concavity on one face indicating a secondary use as a drill bearing. The other two are equipped with suspension holes at the butt end.

The most striking difference between ground slate **knife endblades** from Booth Island and those from Iglulualuit is the presence of many asymmetrical, single-edged specimens from Booth Island. Four formal classes are represented.

Large, single-edged: One knife endblade is 168 mm long, with a large rectangular tang element and a single excurvate cutting margin (Pl. 25, b). The single shoulder is small. It may be unfinished, as the back and base have only been roughly chipped into shape. Five blade fragments also represent large, single-edged knives (Pl. 25, d-f), but little can be deduced of their shape, except that most appear to have been narrower than the complete specimen.

Large, double-edged: Symmetrical, double-edged blades are represented by a basal fragment similar to Iglulualuit specimens (Pl. 25, c), four distal fragments (Pl. 25, g-h, m), and a large, chipped slate preform (Pl. 25, a).

Small, single edged: Two single-edged blades small enough to fit into the simple antler handles described above. Both are symmetrical, with tapering stems and lengths of about 45 mm (Pl. 25, k-1).

Small, double-edged: Two small asymmetrical knife endblades have slightly concave backs, rounded bases, single shoulders, and strongly excurvate cutting margins (Pl. 25, i-j). They are about 55 mm long.

Adzes

A whale bone **adze head** is 126.5 mm long (Pl. 26, b). It has a recessed bed on the bottom surface to accommodate the handle, which was held by a lashing passing through laterally-drilled holes. The blade socket is open on the upper surface, possibly the result of a mended break; the blade was held in place by a lashing passing through drilled holes flanking the blade socket.

An **adze handle** made of wood, presumably spruce, is 380 mm long, with a large triangular lashing hole and a knobbed proximal end (Pl. 26, a). The thickened distal end is too large to fit the recessed bed on the adze head described above.

Other Manufacturing Tools

Drill sockets are very similar to specimens from Langton Bay (Pl. 24, a, f). A complete example is made of antler and is 162

CHAPTER 7: MEN'S TOOLS

mm long, while a second whalebone specimen is broken. One has a gouged, sub-rectangular socket about 18 mm deep, while the other has a split socket of similar depth. Both have a recessed, roughened lashing bed around the socket area, and both have been bevelled proximally for attachment in a split-based shaft.

One **wedge** is made of antler and is 116 mm long (Pl. 26, c), while another is whalebone and only 84 mm long.

A cylindrical whale bone **hammer** is 123 mm long, with heavy pitting and crushing at one end (Pl. 26, e).

Mattocks

Seven complete whale bone mattocks exactly resemble those from Iglulualuit and Okat, with lengths of from 220 to 335 mm. There are also at least two fragmentary specimens.

Snow Knives

Five whalebone snowknives are again like those described from Recent sites, with a curved outline and a single lateral shoulder (Pl. 26, d; Pl. 27, a-b). A sixth is made of two pieces, but likely this only represents the mending of a break between the handgrip and blade sections. The break has been filed flat, and each side pierced by three mending holes. All of the snowknives are broken at the tip, but complete lengths are estimated at about 35 cm.

Discussion

A distinction can be made between the simple endbladed knife handles found at all four sites, and the more elaborate forms represented only at Iglulualuit, Langton Bay, and Okat. In particular, Langton Bay and Okat specimens resemble both historic Alaskan and Copper Inuit knife styles; the latter comparison is particularly striking. There are general similarities with Mackenzie Inuit knife handles as well (see McGhee 1974: 59;

IGLULUALUMIUT PREHISTORY

TABLE 6
Location of Men's Tools: Franklin Bay

	Iglulualuit H 11	H 20	Misc.	Langton	Okat	Booth
Endblade knife handles:						
simple	1			6	7	5
other		2		2	6	
Gravers: fox-tooth		1				
metal-bladed	1	2				2
composite knife						1
Sideblade knife handles				2	1	3
Knife blades:						
large, symmetrical	1	3				5
large, asymmetrical						6
small, symmetrical	4	3				2
small, asymmetrical						2
irregular	1					
Adze Head, simple					4	
Thule style						1
Adze or Pick Handle						1
Flint flakers	1	1				
Drill sockets, small		5				
Drill sockets, large				2		2
Drill spindles		1				
Drill bit					1	
Wedges	3	1	1	4	7	2
Whetstone	1					
Hammer					1	1
Mattocks	2	10			8	9
Snow knives				1	1	6

Morrison 1988a: Pl. 4,a-b). The simple antler handles are a common Thule style (Ford 1959: 167; Morrison 1983a: 128), persisting into the Recent period in many areas, including the Mackenzie Delta (McGhee 1974: 59).

Slate endblades for such knives are present only in the Iglulualuit and Booth Island collections. This is clearly due to collecting priorities, since Stefansson (1914a: 311, 313) mentions finding loose knife blades at both Langton Bay and Okat. Only double-edge, symmetrical blades were found at Iglulualuit, while many of the Booth Island specimens are single-edged, a

CHAPTER 7: MEN'S TOOLS

difference which may be due to chance, since both forms appear widely in comparatively recent Eskimo cultures.

A high frequency of handles with blade slits apparently designed for metal blades is characteristic of all four site collections. Although such blades are not themselves present, socket forms suggest two styles; one flat, and the other long-stemmed, with a heavy, rectangular cross-section. Endblades of the latter type are characteristic of the Coronation Gulf area (Jenness 1946:Fig. 107; Morrison 1983a: Pl. 10,b-c), the source also of the copper from they were presumably made.

Sideblade whittling knife handles from Langton Bay, Okat, and Booth Island are similar. All are of a style too short to be braced against the fore-arm, which is typical of Thule and Recent Western Arctic whittling knives (Murdoch 1892: 159; Mathiassen 1927a: 69; Giddings 1952: 68; McGhee 1974: 60; Morrison 1988a: 46). Historic Copper Inuit whittling knives occasionally used such handles, but a much longer antler handle is more characteristic (Jenness 1946: 101).

The fox-tooth graver found at Iglulualuit is interesting, and likely represents a variant of the familiar beaver-tooth knife, transported north and east beyond the range distribution of beavers. It recalls a moose premolar "chisel" from the Thule culture Washout site on Herschel Island (Yorga 1980: 90). Beaver-tooth knives were also found at Washout (Yorga 1980: 90), and Kittigazuit (McGhee 1974: 62), and are usually associated with western rather than north Alaskan Inupiat (Giddings 1952: 68-68; Giddings 1964: 54). They are absent from the Central and Eastern Arctic. Copper and iron-bladed gravers from Iglulualuit and Booth Island probably served similar functions, as did the composite or splitting-knife represented at Booth Island.

Bow-drill parts, wedges, whetstones, and hammers are all widespread in Eskimo culture. Flint flakers, on the other hand, are more characteristic of Western Eskimo cultures over the past

IGLULUALUMIUT PREHISTORY

thousand years; indeed flint flaking itself is generally rare east of Amundsen Gulf. The antler drill bit-sockets from Langton Bay and Booth Island are unusual and very similar.

Whale bone mattocks occur in some numbers at Iglulualuit, Okat, and Booth Island, and are all similar in lacking drilled or gouged holes for attachment to a handle. They are thus like those from the Western Arctic generally (Ford 1959: 181; Giddings 1952: 79; McGhee 1974: 63), differing from the usual Eastern Thule type (Mathiassen 1927a: 78).

Adze heads of the simple sort without lashing holes were found at Okat. They are also characteristic of Mackenzie Inuit sites like Pt. Atkinson (Mathiassen 1930: 14) and Kittigazuit (McGhee 1974: 63), and occur in Alaska (Giddings 1952: 77; Ford 1959: 178). The typical Thule form has laterally-drilled lashing holes (Mathiassen 1927b: 75; see also Murdoch 1892: Fig. 137), such as was found at Booth Island.

Curved, single-shouldered snow knives like those found at Langton Bay, Okat and Booth Island are ubiquitous in the Amundsen Gulf/Mackenzie area, occurring at the Thule culture Jackson site (Taylor Pl. 3,c), at Barter Island (Mathiassen 1930: Pl. 6, fig. 1), and in Mackenzie Inuit sites like Pt. Atkinson (Mathiassen 1930: Pl. 2,6), Radio Creek (ASC collections), and probably Kittigazuit (McGhee 1974: Pl. 12,h). They also occur in the Eastern Arctic, although a double-shouldered form is usual (Mathiassen 1927b: 65). Alaskan snow knives are rare, late, and quite distinctive in shape (Ford 1959: 143; Stanford 1976: 39).

CHAPTER 8

WOMEN'S TOOLS AND DOMESTIC ITEMS

Iglulualuit

Pottery Vessels

Pottery vessel sherds from Iglulualuit number 141 specimens, but considering the friability of the fabric, this figure can only increase with time. All can be classed as Barrow Plain ware (Griffin and Wilmeth 1964: 275), by far the most common pottery type in Thule to historic contexts in the western Canadian Arctic (see McGhee 1974: 72; Morrison 1983a: 152). Sherds are characteristically soft and friable, with a tendency to crumble and exfoliate. Temper is coarse, and includes sand and grit fragments up to 7.5 mm across. Some also include abundant organic temper such as grass or hair, usually visible as burnt-out casts. Many sherds are covered with burnt grease, and all are brown to black in colour.

Four distinct vessel forms appear to be represented:

Class 1: Perhaps most common are beaker-shaped pots, having a round cross-section, nearly straight sides, and a flat bottom. One large sherd representing about a third of such a pot was found in House 11 (Pl. 35, lower). It has a flat, very slightly flaring rim, stands 133 mm high, and has an estimated diameter of 200 mm. At least six other rims (Pl. 34, a, d) and a number of body sherds suggest a similar shape, with estimated diameters ranging from 200 to 400 mm (mean= 331.4 mm). Rim thicknesses run from 11 to 23 mm (mean= 16.5 mm).

Class 2: A second vessel shape is globular, with sides which curve in two planes, slight shoulders and, probably, a more rounded base. Only two rim sherds represent this form, one of which is everted and slightly flaring, and the other straight in profile (Pl. 34, b-c). It is likely that both represent the same vessel, since both exhibit an otherwise unique trait; the presence of punched holes piercing the rim from the top, and coming out at the bottom of the "lip." These holes were punched while the clay was still soft, and so could not be mending holes, while they are too small (diameter: 2.5 mm) and situated too close to an edge to function as suspension holes. They must be considered decorative, or related to the need to dry the paste properly before firing. The estimated diameter of this vessel is 150 mm. Rim thickness varies between 10.5 and 11 mm.

Class 3: A third vessel is bowl-shaped, with straight, sloping sides and a straight rim. Only a single rim can clearly be attributed to this form (Pl. 34, e). It is 9 mm thick, and has curvature suggesting a bowl with a 200 mm diameter at the mouth.

Class 4: A final vessel form can probably be identified as lamps or kudliks. A concentration of four probable kudliks and part of one beaker-shaped pot was found near the southeastern corner of House 20, all seemingly stacked together. A great deal of burnt grease was in association, along with scraps of leather suggesting that some of the kudliks may have been separated by pieces of leather, or even placed in now partially disintegrated leather bags. Unfortunately, lamps were the most friable pottery at the site, and vessels were badly disintegrated. The best preserved can be reconstructed as a round, flat plate about 300 mm in diameter, with a crudely-modelled raised rim around at least one-third of the circumference. This rim stands about 40 mm high, has a straight, slightly thickened profile, and forms a right-angle with the base of the vessel (Pl. 34, f-g; Pl. 35, upper). Sherd thicknesses vary between 12 and 17 mm. These vessels seem reasonably distinct from the usual saucer-shaped lamp reported from most ceramic sites in the Western Arctic (Ford 1959: Fig. 97), and may instead represent platters or meat trays.

Other Vessel Parts

An antler **bag handle** describes an arc 152 mm long. It has a drilled suspension hole at either end. A shorter wooden specimen is only 110 mm long, and less highly curved. It has notched

CHAPTER 8: WOMEN'S TOOLS

rather than pierced ends.

Two antler **vessel rims** are each about 20 mm wide, with a medial row of pegged holes for attachment. In one case the in situ pegs are of wood, in the other of antler.

Hide Scrapers

Fifteen chipped quartzite **endscrapers** are sub-triangular to nearly rectangular in outline, with tapering or parallel-sided stems and rounded bits (Pl. 28, h-m). The cross-section through the bit is usually plano-convex, but most specimens have been worked bifacially. Lengths range from 24 to 41 mm (mean: 31.5 mm); thicknesses from 6 to 11 mm (mean: 8 mm); and chords widths from 20 to 33 mm (mean: 27 mm).

Twenty **spall scrapers** from Iglulualuit are made on tabular pieces of sandstone or slate, and have rough, bifacially chipped edges along some part of the circumference. Few appear to have been intentionally shaped, so that outline form varies greatly. Most show some definite evidence of edge wear, and are hand sized or slightly larger (maximum length: 173 mm). Thicknesses run between 7 and 18 mm.

Ulus

A single **ulu handle** is made of wood (Pl. 36, b). It is cylindrical in shape, slightly curved, with a blade slit 68 mm long and 6.5 mm wide. It evidently held a heavy stone blade. The total length is 110 mm.

Eighteen loose **ulu blades** are mostly fragmentary. All are made of ground slate, ranging from a purplish or ox-blood colour, through black, to a greenish-grey. None have rivet or lashing holes for attachment to a handle. Working margins are mostly curved, and thicknesses vary from 3 to 6.5 mm. Only four are complete; three of these are of a similar trianguloid or trapezoid outline, with chipped, sometimes slightly notched, backs (Pl. 28,

IGLULUALUMIUT PREHISTORY

a-c). Length of the working margin ranges from 55.5 mm to 68 mm. It is likely that they were hafted, and they generally resemble "Class 1" blades from Kittigazuit (McGhee 1974: 68). The fourth complete ulu blade is rectangular, with sawed lateral edges, and a width of 63 mm. It could not have been hafted, but shows polish on edge facets suggestive of its being used while presumably hand held. There are also two chipped blanks.

Miscellaneous Domestic Items

Two **marrow spatulas** are made of bone, in one case a caribou metatarsal splinter (Pl. 28, f), in the other a ringed seal fibula. Both have spatulate and well worn distal ends, and are fairly rough-made, without carved hand grips, etc.

Two caribou scapulae with scraping planes on a cut lateral margin resemble ethnographic **fish scalers** (Pl. 28, e). Similar tools appear widely in the Western Arctic (Giddings 1952: 39; Hall 1971: 33; Stanford 1976: 55; Morrison 1983a: 145).

The end of a broken antler **spoon** shows a line of drilled holes along the present break, suggestive of mending holes (Pl. 28, d).

A pebble of porous, volcanic rock has been split and polished along the split face. It may represent a **burnishing stone**, used for smoothing any of a variety of materials.

A bird long bone-tube is too small to have functioned as a needle case, being 166 mm long but only 7.5 mm in diameter. It is presumably a **drinking tube** like those found in most Eskimo cultures.

Of six **awls or bodkins**, two are long-bone splinters and four are of antler. All but one come to a generally sharp point such as would be useful for punching holes through leather, etc. The exception has too wide a point for piercing, but heavy tip polish does suggest some function such as incising a design in birch bark. In turn, this tool is incised with a rough latter motif on

CHAPTER 8: WOMEN'S TOOLS

one face.

Finally, a number of leather scraps, and leather and baleen knots were found, but the only recognizable piece of clothing is a small section from the crimped toe of a **boot or kamik**.

Games, Amulets, and Ornaments

A bearded seal humerus has a cut groove for a line, and a narrow drilled hole. It was evidently used in the cup-and-pin game of **ajagaq**.

A wooden **carving of a bowhead whale** is 103 mm long (Pl. 36, a). It is carved in the round, but lacks incised features. It is similar to ethnographic specimens from Pt. Barrow, and may have been similarly used as a whaling amulet (Murdoch 1892: 402).

A **toy harpoon head** is made of antler, and faithfully depicts the Nunagiak barbed type (Pl. 28, g). It is 40 mm long, and made of antler. The Nunagiak barbed harpoon head is also represented by a full sized blank at Iglulualuit.

An cylindrical antler **pendant** 40 mm long is encircled by four incised lines, and terminates in a tiny pair of "ears." Another possible example consists of a narrow, flat piece of ivory 83 mm long (Pl. 28, q). It has a drilled suspension hole at the wider end, and comes to a narrow, spatulate tip at the other. It is decorated with a rather crudely incised criss-cross pattern. The spatulate tip could have some specific function, for instance as a feather setter in arrow manufacture. Another ivory specimen is also illustrated (Pl. 28, p). Two bone pendants consist of a drilled bear phalanx, and the drilled proximal end of a large canid (wolf?) left fourth metatarsal (Pl. 28, n-o).

An ovate piece of antler 43 mm long has a drilled central hole (Pl. 28, r). It may have functioned as a button or **clothing toggle**. A second, larger specimen is 70 mm long, and may have functioned as a small handle.

IGLULUALUMIUT PREHISTORY

Langton Bay

Vessel Parts

A **bag or quiver handle** is 280 mm long, broken, and probably made of antler (Pl. 29, f). It is very well finished, with a pair of suspension holes at either end, and a plano-convex cross-section. On the upper face is an incised stick-figure holding a what appears to be a walking stick or staff. A much cruder antler bag handle is 155 mm long, with a notch at one end and a drilled hole at the other.

Antler **vessel rims** between 20 and 25 mm wide are similar to those from Iglulualuit.

Hide Scrapers

Scraper handles consist of short antler sections with broad sockets up to 36 mm wide cut in one end (Pl. 29, c-e). There are no scraper blades in the collection.

Ulus

Two antler **ulu handles** are of the cylindrical shape, 39 and 68.5 mm long (Pl. 29, a-b). Each has a small suspension hole in the back, perhaps to hold a sharpener. The smaller specimen is particularly similar to an ulu handle from Kittigazuit (McGhee 1974: 69). Again blades of any sort are absent.

Miscellaneous Domestic Items

A curved antler tine 120 mm long has a blade slit cut along one lateral margin toward the middle of the piece (Pl. 29, h). The blade slit is only 38 mm long, and would have held a metal blade. Nearly identical tools were used by historic north Alaskans as **baleen shaves** (Murdoch 1892: 173).

Two rough **marrow spatulas** were made on caribou metatarsal splinters.

Rough **awls and bodkins** were made of both bone and antler,

CHAPTER 8: WOMEN'S TOOLS

and take a number of expedient forms.

An ivory **thimble holder** takes the classic toggle shape (Pl. 29, g). The concave under-surface has two drilled holes on each "wing"; these would presumably have held small decorative inlays.

Ornaments

Pendants come in a multiplicity of forms. One is a large canid incisor with a suspension hole drilled through the root end (Pl. 29, j). Another is an unidentified tooth cut in half and grooved for suspension (Pl. 29, k), while a third is also of ivory and drilled from several directions (Pl. 29, i). Finally a bird bone tube with a diameter of 7.5 mm and a length of 36 mm is too small to have functioned as either a needle case or drinking tube, and so might be considered a tubular bead (Pl. 29, l).

Okat

Vessel Parts

A curved antler **bag handle** has drilled holes at either end, and an incised spurred line motif on one face (Pl. 31, a). It is 240 mm long.

Bone and antler strips about 20 mm wide and up to 300 mm long have a line of drilled holes along their length, and seem to represent **vessel rims** like those from other sites.

Hide Scrapers

Eight **scraper handles** consist of short lengths of antler with sockets 15 to 34 mm wide cut in one end (Pl. 30, g-j; Pl. 31, b-d). Most are curved, or take advantage of a fork in the antler to provide a hand hold. They are similar to Langton Bay specimens.

Quartzite **endscrapers** for such handles are sub-triangular in plan, with poorly defined stems (Pl. 30, k-l). All show some bifacial chipping at the distal end, and fit into the narrower of

IGLULUALUMIUT PREHISTORY

the handle sockets described above. Lengths range from 31.5 to 43 mm, and chord widths from 28 to 33 mm.

Ulus

Six antler **ulu handles** are of roughly cylindrical shape, sometimes slightly curved, and sometimes so short that they are nearly rectangular in outline (Pl. 30, a-f). All have a blade slit along most of one long margin, and an ovate cross-section. None are decorated, but two have the small drilled holes exhibited by Langton Bay specimens. Lengths range from 49 to 93.5 mm. A final ulu handle is rectangular and very flat, only 39 mm long, and again provided with a small hole to hold a sharpener (Pl. 31, e). At least four could only have accommodated a metal blade.

A single slate **ulu blade** fragment is too small to type (Pl. 30, m).

Miscellaneous Domestic Items

A fragment from a wooden **cutting board** is 12.5 mm thick. One face shows a large number of cut marks.

Two fragmentary **marrow spatulas** are well finished but, like those from other Franklin Bay sites, lack edge scalloping or other special features (Pl. 31, f).

A one-piece antler **knife** 271 mm long has sharp lateral edges, and a flat cross-section (Pl. 31, h). It may have been used to chop snow, or in some other domestic function.

A complete antler **ladle** has a shallow bowl measuring 59 x 101 mm, with a short, square stem equipped with three attachment holes (Pl. 31, g). A second broken specimen, also of antler, has a one-piece handle.

There are also three rough bone and antler **awls** in the Okat collection.

CHAPTER 8: WOMEN'S TOOLS

Booth Island

Pottery Vessels

Only five pottery sherds are represented in the Booth Island collection, but this is almost certainly a reflection of the interests of the excavator rather than a true indication of the frequency of pottery at the site. All are rims, and probably come from the same vessel, which is of typical Barrow Plain ware. The vessel appears to have been of the globular or Class 2 shape, with a slight shoulder and rounded sides (Pl. 33, 1). The rim has a deep exterior channel above the shoulder, a rim thickness averaging about 17 mm, and an estimated diameter at the mouth of about 200 mm. Temper includes grit up to 5.5 mm across, and the burned casts of some organic fibre, probably grass or hair.

Other Vessel Parts

A crude **bag or basket handle** was made on a comparatively straight, roughened piece of antler 152 mm long. It has holes drilled at either end for suspension (Pl. 33, a).

Hide Scrapers

Four quartzite **endscrapers** of the usual form are present (Pl. 33, g-j). Lengths range from 42 to 47 mm, thicknesses from 9 to 12 mm, and chord widths from 29.5 to 40 mm.

A **bone beamer or two-handed scraper** was made from the anterior half of a coronally-split caribou metacarpal (Pl. 32, a). There is clear evidence of sharpening and polishing along both cut edges.

Ulus

Four antler **ulu handles** represent three different shape classes. One specimen is more or less cylindrical, like Iglulualuit, Langton Bay and Okat specimens, with an ovate cross-section and a blade slit along one long margin (Pl. 32, c). On

IGLULUALUMIUT PREHISTORY

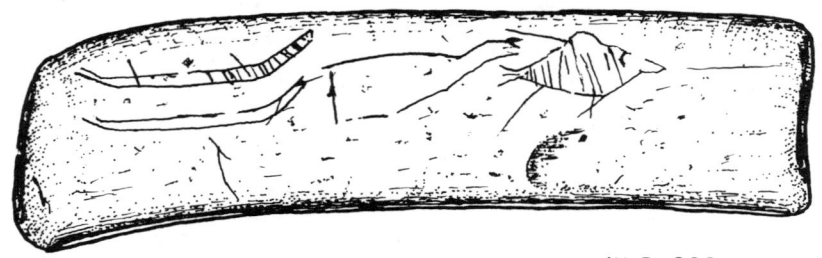

IX·D·292

FIGURE 8
DECORATED ULU HANDLE FROM BOOTH ISLAND

one face is incised a hunting scene, depicting two kayaks in pursuit of a swimming caribou (?) and a seal (Fig. 8). It would have held a metal blade, and is 102.5 mm long. Two handles are D-shaped, with a rounded back, a concave blade margin, and a flat cross-section. One is large (length: 108.5 mm) and would have again held a metal blade. The other is shorter (51 mm), and was evidently associated with a particular slate blade (Pl. 32, d & e). The final ulu handle is similar in shape to these two, except that the back is thickened and there is a central "finger hole" (Pl. 32, b). It is 107.5 mm long, and the blade margin has been slit to accommodate two metal blades, 49 and 20 mm long, respectively.

CHAPTER 8: WOMEN'S TOOLS

Ninety-seven **ulu blades** or fragments were recovered from Booth Island. All are of slate, and are generally similar in colour and thickness to those from Iglulualuit. One complete example (Pl. 32, e)was found still in its handle; it is short (only 67 mm long), with a curved blade margin and a rectangular chipped back. A broken specimen is similar, although slightly larger (Pl. 32, h). Both somewhat resemble the trianguloid Iglulualuit specimens, but differ in having a broader, more rectangular tang. They at least could have been hafted, which is not apparently true of any of the other blades in the collection. Another complete blade (Pl. 32, g) has a comparatively straight cutting edge and a elongated, tang-like back, which would have provided a hand grip. Another (Pl. 32, i) is asymmetric, with a rounded working margin and a snapped back. All other specimens are fragmentary, or so irregular in outline that it cannot be determined whether they are complete or broken. Common traits include the absence of a clearly-defined edge bevel, and the presence of back and side margins which have been snapped or, more commonly, chipped into shape, without grinding. Lateral notches are absent or at best very shallow, and there are no rivet or lashing holes. Many specimens, in fact, are so crude they consist only of a slate flake with one edge ground sharp.

Toys and Ornaments

A **toy harpoon head** represents the Nunagiak barbed type, and is very similar to a toy from Iglulualuit (Pl. 33, b). It is made of antler, and is 56 mm long.

A beautifully carved ivory **pendant** is of conical shape, with a tiny suspension hole at the proximal end, and an ball-shaped terminal at the other end (Pl. 33, c). It is encircled by a pair of incised hatched lines, and is 45.5 mm long. A carved antler **bead** is crudely modelled, with a diameter of 11 mm, and a gouged, central hole (Pl. 33, d).

IGLULUALUMIUT PREHISTORY

An antler comb has an hour-glass shape, with an interior spurred-line border and seven teeth (Pl. 33, e).

Discussion

Pottery vessels are characteristic of Thule culture and Recent sites from Coronation Gulf west. The absence of pottery sherds from Langton Bay and Okat, and their comparative rarity at Booth Island, is due to collecting priorities, since Stefansson (1914a: 312-314) mentions abundant pottery at Langton Bay and Okat. The available pottery from Iglulualuit and Booth Island is all of Barrow Plain ware (Griffin and Wilmeth 1964: 275), by far the most common ware type in most of the Western Arctic, particularly by late prehistoric times (McGhee 1974: 72; Morrison 1983a: 152). A high frequency of surface decoration, however, does distinguish the pottery from the Kobuk River area (Giddings 1952: 93-103). Because later Arctic pottery is invariably friable and usually in an advanced state of disintegration, it is difficult to systematically compare vessel forms with those of other sites and regions. Class 1 beaker-shaped pots are the best represented at Iglulualuit, and seem very similar to the usual pot form employed in north Alaska (Griffin and Wilmeth 1964: 275-6; Ford 1959: 201; Stanford 1976: 57). Rounded Class 2 vessels, also found at Iglulualuit, but more common at Booth Island, are instead characteristic of Thule pottery in the Coronation Gulf area (Morrison 1983a: 153), and in west Alaska (Giddings 1952: Fig. 40). Both vessel forms seem present at the Mackenzie Inuit sites of Kittigazuit and Radio Creek (McGhee 1974: 72, 81).

Vessels others than those of pottery are poorly represented in Franklin Bay sites. A few of the sites produced bag handles, and all yielded antler strips with drilled holes, presumed to be side or reinforcement pieces. Absent are the baleen and wooden bowls and platters found in many areas.

Quartzite endscrapers of typical Western Arctic form (see

CHAPTER 8: WOMEN'S TOOLS

TABLE 7
Location of Women's Tools and Domestic Items: Franklin Bay

	Iglulualuit H 11	H 20	Misc.	Langton	Okat	Booth
Pottery rim sherds:						
vessel Class 1	5	2				
vessel Class 2	2					5
vessel Class 3	1					
misc. rim sherds	3	4				
Pottery lamps		4				
Pottery body sherds	46	23				
Bag handles		1	1	2	1	1
Vessel rims, antler	2			4	4	
Scraper handles				3	8	
Endscrapers, quartzite	8	7			3	4
Spall scrapers	11	9				
Beamer						1
Ulu handle: cylindrical		1		2	6	1
flat					1	
D-shaped						2
holed						1
Ulu blades: haftable		3				2
irregular/frag.	5	10			1	93
blanks	1	1				6
Cutting board				1		
Baleen shave			1			
Marrow spatulas		2		2	2	
Antler knife					1	
"Fish scalers"	1	1				
Spoon and ladles	1				2	
Burnishing stone		1				
Awls/bodkins	2	4		7	3	
Drinking tube	1					
Thimble holder				1		
Boot fragment		1				
Ajagaq	1					
Whale effigy		1				
Toy harpoon heads		1				1
Pendants, beads	1	4		4		2
Togggles	1		1			
Comb						1

IGLULUALUMIUT PREHISTORY

McGhee 1974: 67; Ford 1959: 193) are common. Also well represented are simple antler scraper handles, similar to specimens from the Mackenzie Inuit (McGhee 1974: 68) and from north and west Alaska (Murdoch 1892: Fig. 298; Hall 1971: 34). Spall scrapers appear only in the Iglulualuit collection, but they too are associated with Mackenzie Inuit (McGhee 1974: 68; Morrison 1988a: 53), and with west Alaskans (Giddings 1952: 82). Their absence from Langton Bay, Okat, and Booth Island is probably a reflection of collecting techniques, since spall scrapers are unprepossessing tools, and easily missed by the amateur excavator. A single bone beamer was found at Booth Island.

Ulu handles from the three Recent sites take a similar cylindrical form, with long blade slits which in many cases could only have accommodated a metal blade. Similar antler handles occur widely in the Western Arctic, but are quite different from the typical Copper Inuit form, which was invariably equipped with a separate tang element (see Jenness 1946: 80). Wooden handles like the one from Iglulualuit find a more specific comparison with the Mackenzie Inuit (McGhee 1974: 69). Booth Island yielded four handle types, but again these occur widely within the context of Thule culture (Mathiassen 1927b: 84-89; Mathiassen 1930: Pl. 4, fig. 19, Pl. 10, fig. 9; Ford 1959: 186; McGhee 1972: Pl. IV,c; Stanford 1976: 52; Morrison 1983a: 138; Giddings and Anderson 1986: 80). Loose slate blades from all four sites appear to have been mostly unhaftable, a trait reminescent of the slate blades from Thule sites in Coronation Gulf (Morrison 1983a: 136).

Resembling a small ulu, a long, curved baleen shave appears in the Okat collection, similar to specimens from the Mackenzie Inuit (Mathiassen 1930: 38; McGhee 1974: Pl. 21,j) and north Alaska (Ford 1959: 181).

Miscellaneous domestic items are similar from all four sites, and include a fragmentary cutting board, fish scalers, marrow spatulas, spoons and ladles, a burnishing stone, and a

CHAPTER 8: WOMEN'S TOOLS

drinking tube. Sewing gear is limited to rough awls and bodkins, except for a winged thimble-holder of typical form from Langton Bay. An simple antler knife from Okat may have been used for chopping snow. It resembles bone knives for squeezing water, known from Recent times at Pt. Barrow (Mathiassen 1930: Pl. 8, fig. 8; Ford 1959: Fig. 47), except that the blade is flat rather than curved in cross-section.

Items of adornment, amulets, games, and toys are comparatively few in number. Most sites produced a few pendants. Toys are limited to miniature harpoon heads, and a bearded seal humerus used in playing ajagak, a cup-and-pin game. The lone comb is a rather crude antler specimen from Booth Island, with an hour-glass outline, and typical Thule ornamentation. Similar rectangular combs with slightly concave sides and tops are widespread (Mathiassen 1927b: 113; Morrison 1983a: 160; Giddings and Anderson 1986: 52). A wooden whale effigy from Iglulualuit depicts a bowhead whale, and underscores ethnographic evidence of Recent whaling in Franklin Bay (Stefansson 1914a: 332).

CHAPTER 9

CHRONOLOGY AND CULTURAL POSITION

The Thule Period

Dating Booth Island

Like other Thule sites between the Alaskan border and Coronation Gulf, it is difficult to date Booth Island accurately. This is due in part to conflicting horizon slopes, and a history of research which has generally concentrated on Alaska, on one hand, and the greater Baffin Island/eastern High Arctic area on the other. As a case in point, a harpoon head collection like that from Booth Island includes a preponderance of Thule types 2 and 3, with some of the latter tending toward the Sicco subtype. In the Eastern Arctic, such an assemblage would be considered "Classic" Thule, assigned to a period between about A.D. 1000 and 1200 (see McCartney 1977). But in the Western Arctic it could date much later, as late as A.D. 1400.

There is some reason for preferring the later, Western Thule cross-date. Stylistically, the Booth Island collection resembles Western Thule more than it does material from sites like Naujan (Mathiassen 1927a) or Silumiut (McCartney 1977) in the northern Hudson Bay area. While not identical to Alaskan assemblages, it does share Western styles of fish hook shanks and arrowhead tangs, chipped-stone endblades and scrapers, and above all, pottery. This general stylistic affinity suggests that the most profitable comparison is with Western Arctic material.

Within the range of variation encompassed by Alaskan Thule, Booth Island perhaps most greatly resembles assemblages from western Alaska, particularly Ekseavik in the Kobuk River sequence (Giddings 1952), or late Western Thule on the Cape Krusenstern beaches (Giddings and Anderson 1986). Fish-hook shanks are an important link, absent from both north Alaska and the East, and apparently not present earlier than the Ekseavik/late Western Thule phase in western Alaska (Giddings 1952: 39; Giddings and Anderson 1986: 71). Arrowhead similarities are also significant,

CHAPTER 9: CHRONOLOGY AND CULTURAL POSITION

including the first appearance of the late squared shoulder, and the predominance of the ringed tang form (Giddings 1952: 45; Giddings and Anderson 1986: 70). The harpoon heads, while undoubtedly early by Eastern Arctic standards, are not necessarily so by comparison with Western sites. The predominance of open socket forms, however, does clearly indicate a date prior to perhaps the mid-15th century, since they are quite different from the later, Kotzebue phase heads (Giddings 1952: 53; Giddings and Anderson 1986: 55). Again, the Ekseavik/late Western Thule harpoon heads provide a close comparison. Thule types 2 and 3 predominate, while the early Sicco subtype of Thule type 3 does apparently persist in western Alaska as late as A.D. 1400. Slender, decorated Barrow closed socket harpoon heads like the Booth Island specimen also occur (Giddings 1952: 54-55; Giddings and Anderson 1986: 70). There are a few post-Ekseavik traits in the Booth Island collection, particularly the spurring seen on some arrowhead tangs, and the fairly common appearance of drilled lashing slots and rivet holes on harpoon heads. These are traits which were developed much earlier in the Eastern Arctic, and their appearance in the West was once ascribed to a "return Thule migration" (Collins 1937: 309). While this suggestion is no longer tenable (see Morrison 1983a: 23), they are clearly traits with an east-west horizon slope, and could be expected to be earlier in the Amundsen Gulf area than in Alaska. In short, there are enough similarities between Booth Island and Ekseavik/late Western Thule to suggest that they date at least in large part to about the same general period; around A.D. 1350-1400.

The Clachan Phase

While Booth Island shows clear stylistic affinities with the Western Thule culture of Alaska, its closest similarities are with other sites in the western Canadian Arctic. It seems to be one of several sites representing a reasonably distinctive variant of

IGLULUALUMIUT PREHISTORY

Thule culture known as the Clachan phase, after the western Coronation Gulf site upon which it was first defined (Morrison 1983a). As is clear from the previous chapter, there are important similarities between the Booth Island and western Coronation Gulf assemblages, including rounded pottery vessels, and especially the harpoon heads. The Clachan open socket harpoon head is the most abundant type at the Clachan type-site, and has a geographic distribution which is almost entirely limited to the area between that site and the mouth of the Mackenzie River. It is the third most popular type at Booth Island. The Clachan assemblage also includes abundant Thule type 2 and 3 harpoon heads, spanning the same range of variation as those from Booth Island. Important similarities here include Sicco-like Thule 3 specimens, with the otherwise unusual combination of ornamental sideblade slots and drilled lashing holes and/or endblade rivet holes, and the presence of sharp shoulder spurs on some of the Thule 2s. This latter trait seems to be unique to Booth Island, Clachan, and several of the later Franklin Bay sites. The Nuwuk and Barrow types also appear in low frequencies. Antler arrowheads show a similar mix of "late," "Eastern" spurred tangs, and Western Arctic tang types such as ringed and conically knobbed. The higher frequencies of weak shouldered knobbed tangs, and conically knobbed tangs, in the Clachan collection suggest that that site is slightly older than Booth Island, perhaps by 50 or 100 years.

If Clachan is the most similar large assemblage to Booth Island, there are nonetheless differences. Some of these may be temporal in nature, such as the absence of fish-hook shanks at Clachan. Others may be more apparent than real, the product of differences in sample size (the Clachan assemblage is much larger), or of Mr. Hadley's collection strategy. Copper tools, for instance, are absent from the Booth Island collection, but abundant at Clachan (see Morrison 1987). However, many of the knife and ulu handles from Booth Island were certainly used with

FIGURE 9

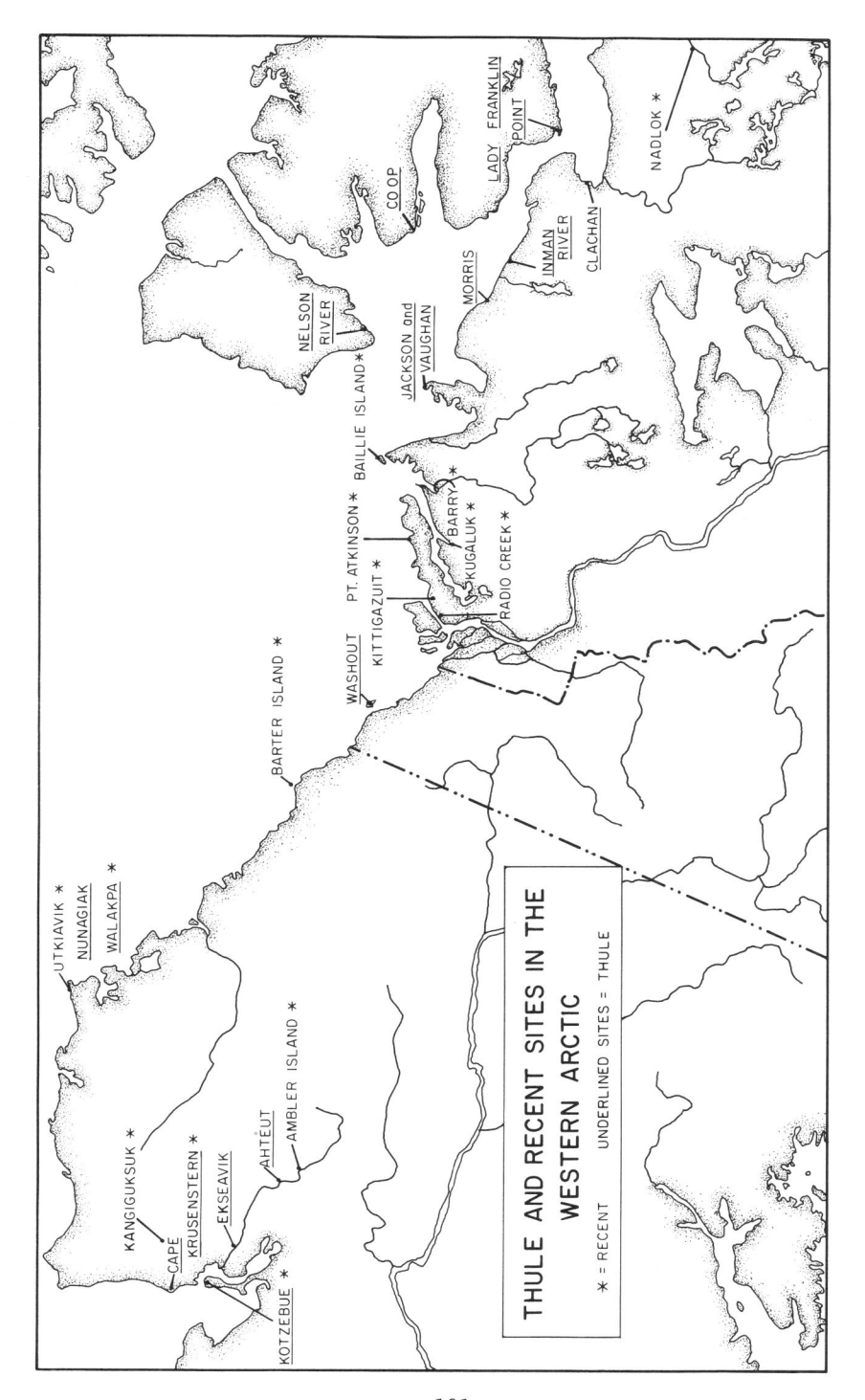

THULE AND RECENT SITES IN THE WESTERN ARCTIC

IGLULUALUMIUT PREHISTORY

metal blades.

In the area between Booth Island and Clachan are several Thule sites which have been briefly tested, including Jackson and Vaughan at Cape Parry (Taylor 1972), the Morris site at Tysoe Point (Taylor 1972), and an unamed site at the mouth of the Inman River (ASC Old Catalogue). All four fall within the range of variation defined by Clachan and Booth Island, and include in their inventories Clachan open and closed socket harpoon heads, Thule type 2 and Sicco-like Thule type 3 harpoon heads, fish-shaped fish-hook shanks, abundant pottery and copper, and arrowheads with knobbed, conically knobbed, ringed and spurred tangs. The presence of single-shouldered snow knives and the unusual flat B1a harpoon head type at Jackson and Vaughan make those two sites particularly similar to Booth Island, only a few dozen kilometres to the west. Taylor (1972) reports rectangular, Western-Thule style wooden houses at Jackson and Vaughan. Nothing is directly known of the houses at Booth Island, but they were presumably similar. This is another variable in Clachan phase Thule, since houses in the western Coronation Gulf area are rounded in plan, and use less wood (Morrison 1983a: Fig. 8), reflecting differences in the availability of drift wood. The sole "acceptable" radiocarbon date from Jackson essayed at A.D. 1350±105 (I-2052, uncorrected; Wilmeth 1978: 36), which agrees well with the suggested cross-date for Booth Island.

Looking to the west of Booth Island, it is important to note that no Thule age site has yet been identified in the area between Franklin Bay and the Yukon border. Given recent intensive reconnaissance in this area (LeBlanc 1987), the absence or at least great rarity of Thule sites here is probably real, and the product of destruction through land subsidence. West of the Mackenzie, the nearest Thule site is probably Whitefish Station (NeVc-1), briefly tested over 30 years ago (MacNeish 1956). But the nearest significant collection comes from Washout, on Herschel

CHAPTER 9: CHRONOLOGY AND CULTURAL POSITION

Island (Yorga 1980). Most artifact similarities shared with Booth Island are of a general Western Thule nature, such as the abundant pottery, knobbed tanged arrowheads, and the use of chipped stone for endblades and scrapers. Washout also produced a fair number of copper artifacts, arrowheads with spurred tangs, harpoon heads with both slotted and drilled lashing holes, and fish-hook shanks and single-shouldered snow knives like those from Booth Island. The distinctive Clachan harpoon head types are absent, however, as are Sicco-like harpoon heads with ornamental sideblade slots and drilled lashing holes. The presence of Nunagiak and Kilimatavik harpoon heads, and fish-hook shanks, suggest that House 2 at Washout is as recent as Booth Island, while House 1 appears to be significantly older. While not explicitly included in the Clachan phase, the Washout site is nonetheless closely related. If Thule sites are ever found and excavated from the intervening Mackenzie Delta area, Washout may be found to be simply the westernmost point in a range of geographically related stylistic variation spanning the western Canadian Arctic.

The Clachan phase, thus defined, includes sites at the western end of Coronation Gulf and along the southern shore of Amundsen Gulf. Several Thule sites have been excavated from northern Amundsen Gulf, including the Cape Kellett and Nelson River sites from southern Banks Island (Manning 1956; Arnold and Stimmell 1983), and the Memorana and Coop sites on the western coast of Victoria Island (McGhee 1972; Le Mouel and Le Mouel 1987). Unfortunately, none of these sites except Memorana has been published in detail. Memorana seems fairly distinct from the Clachan phase, although the assemblage does include some pottery. The arrowheads, however, all have spurred tangs, and the harpoon head collection is dominated by an unusual variant of Thule type 2 not found further south. Clachan type harpoon heads are absent, as are the distinctive Sicco-like harpoon heads with drilled lashing and rivet holes. Judging from preliminary reports the other three sites are all very early. Only Coop has produced a Clachan type harpoon head, and that but a single specimen from the later levels of the site (M. Le Mouel, personal communication).

The relationship between the Clachan phase and the general Thule occupation of Arctic Canada is slowly being clarified by work in the eastern Arctic, particularly that of McCullough (1986) on Ellesmere Island. There is growing evidence of at least two reasonably discrete migrations from Alaska, each of which in itself was probably not a simple, single event. The earliest and probably most important is marked in particular by the Natchuk harpoon head type, an early form of Thule type 2 (Ford 1959: 83). Sites with Natchuk heads include Washout, where there is a surface find (Yorga 1980: 62), the Nelson River site on the southeastern corner of Banks Island (Arnold and Stimmell 1983: 1), Semmler's Lady Franklin Point collection from the western end of Coronation Gulf (Taylor 1963; Morrison 1983a: 218-221), the M1 site on Cornwallis Island (Collins 1952: 51), and the Maxwell Bay site on the southern coast of Devon Island (Taylor 1963). The distribution of these sites suggests a general occupation of the Arctic mainland coast and the Middle Arctic Islands from Parry Channel south, probably in the 11th or 12th centuries A.D. The stylistically distinctive Ruin Island phase from eastern Ellesmere Island and adjacent northwest Greenland can probably be distinguished as the product of a separate, later migration, restricted to the High Arctic islands. Ruin Island assemblages lack the Natchuk harpoon head type, but do include Thule type 2 and Sicco harpoon heads. A series of radiocarbon dates suggests a date of about A.D. 1200 for Ruin Island (McCullough 1986).

Reasons for this series of population movements are imperfectly understood, although they are often considered a cultural response to the warm Neo-Atlantic climatic optimum, and a resultant extension in the range of bowhead whales (McGhee 1969/70). Recently McGhee (1984c) has suggested that meteoric and

CHAPTER 9: CHRONOLOGY AND CULTURAL POSITION

later Norse iron sources in western Greenland may also have been powerful inducements to migration. However, it can be noted that the earliest migrations took people into some places where whales were absent, such as Coronation Gulf. Moreover, the occupation of the iron-producing areas of Greenland and the adjacent eastern High Arctic appear to have been later than that of areas further south. Population and social pressure in the northwest Alaskan homeland may instead have been the primary motivations.

The Clachan phase appears to represent a development from the original Low Arctic migration along the mainland coast of western Canada. This placement seems fairly secure, with pioneering-phase Natchuk harpoon head sites bracketing the Amundsen Gulf area; at Herschel Island, southern Banks Island, and western Coronation Gulf. Communication with developing Eastern Thule culture appears to have been fairly minimal, although Coronation Gulf copper appears in some Eastern Arctic sites (Mathiassen 1927a: 60), and Eastern Thule traits like spurred arrowhead tangs and shouldered snow knives appear in Clachan phase sites. The use of soapstone for vessels and lamps, however, was not adopted, despite good soapstone sources within the range of the Clachan phase. Communication with Alaska, particularly western Alaska, appears to have been more important, so that the appearance of fish-hook shanks, and changes in the form of arrowheads and harpoon heads are mirrored in the Amundsen-Coronation Gulf area. A developed form of the Clachan phase probably appeared by the thirteenth century A.D. In the far eastern part of its range, the Clachan phase underlies the development of the historic Copper Inuit (Morrison 1983a).

Just as the stylistic aspects of the Clachan phase appear to vary within certain limits as one travels east or west, so too do subsistence practices vary in response to different environmental conditions, and possibly changes in technology. At present this is more an assumption than a tested observation, since faunal

IGLULUALUMIUT PREHISTORY

material is available only from Coronation Gulf sites. There, in the absence of larger sea mammals, subsistence focused on caribou and seal. Several lines of evidence suggest that breathing-hole sealing was little practised, and that instead open-water and ice-edge hunting were important (Morrison 1983b). The breathing-hole seal indicator from Booth Island is similar to historic specimens, and suggests the beginnings of effective breathing-hole sealing in the western Canadian Arctic at a date only slightly later than the occupation of the western Coronation Gulf sites. The Booth Island Thule people were probably also whalers in the classic Thule tradition, since they lived within even the modern range of bowhead whales (Davis et al. 1980). Stefansson mentions "numerous" abandoned villages at Booth Island and at Cape Parry, one of which is probably the Booth Island site. The bone debris suggested to Stefansson that the inhabitants "lived chiefly by sealing, but also partly by bowhead whaling" (Stefansson 1914a: 16). Taylor (1972: 13, 26) also presents evidence of whaling at the Jackson and Vaughan sites.

The Recent Period in Franklin Bay

Dating

The chronological picture presented by Iglulualuit, Langton Bay, and Okat is somewhat ambiguous. All produced harpoon head assemblages dominated by closed socket forms, which indicates dates after about A.D. 1450, contemporaneous with Kittigazuit (McGhee 1974) and the Kotzebue culture of west Alaska (Giddings 1952; Giddings and Anderson 1986). There are few other chronological markers.

Only Iglulualuit has been radiocarbon dated. It has produced six dates, all on caribou bone or antler. Three from House 20 assayed at A.D. 1410±70 (S-2948), A.D. 1470±70 (S-2947), and A.D. 1520±120 (S-3002), while two from House 11 produced dates of A.D. 1700±205 (S-3003) and A.D. 1760±70 (S-3004). A sixth

CHAPTER 9: CHRONOLOGY AND CULTURAL POSITION

sample, an antler surface-find unrelated to either excavated house, was dated A.D. 1690±100 (RIDDL-543; LeBlanc 1987: 124). Together these dates suggest that the site was occupied over most of the Recent period, with House 20 dating to the early part of the period, and House 11 to the late part. A similarly long occupational history has been reported from other large Recent sites in the western Canadian Arctic, including Pt. Atkinson and Kittigazuit (Mathiassen 1930: 18; McGhee 1974: 83-85). However, it must be noted that the apparent age difference between Houses 11 and 20 is not clearly reflected in their artifact assemblages. Ovate, tangless chipped stone arrow points, for instance, are a possible early chronological marker at Iglulualuit, comparing best with those from basal Kittigazuit and the earlier parts of the Kobuk River sequence. Yet such arrow points occur in similar frequencies in both houses (see Table 4). Harpoon head types, arrowhead tang forms, and other traits also seem essentially similar.

Only the Langton Bay site produced a few specifically Thule artifact types, including several open socket harpoon heads (Thule type 2 and Clachan), and arrowheads with ringed or conically knobbed tangs. Unfortunately, they could be evidence of stratigraphic mixing as easily as of a early or transitional status for the site. Aside from these few artifacts, the Langton Bay collection is very similar to that from Okat, and that site, at least, appears to cross-date very well with the post-A.D. 1600 levels at Kittigazuit. None of these sites is historic, although iron is present or its use inferred since Thule times.

The Iglulualumiut

The Recent period in Franklin Bay spans about 400 years, from some time in the fifteenth century to after A.D. 1800. It is currently represented by three sites, whose artifact assemblages clearly indicate a Western Eskimo cultural affiliation. Some of

IGLULUALUMIUT PREHISTORY

these artifacts, such as fish-hook shanks and abundant Barrow Plain Ware pottery, are found also in the preceeding Thule period. Other traits, such as the cruciform houses at Iglulualuit, may be recent introductions, and point particularly to the Mackenzie Inuit. Absent are Central Eskimo traits such as tanged ulus and soapstone vessels, while artifacts such as the long, loose harpoon foreshafts and heavy harpoon socketpieces are again of specifically Western form. The dominant harpoon head type, Nuwuk/Barrow, is common from west Alaska to Queen Maud Gulf, but other, rarer types again point specifically to the Mackenzie Delta area, or to Alaska. Included are the Brower, Nunagiak barbed and Kotzebue 1 types. Way of life, too, clearly distinguishes the Franklin Bay people from Copper or other Central Inuit, and allies them with the people of the Mackenzie Delta region. That they lived in "permanent" log and sod houses and hunted bowhead whales are major distinguishing factors.

For the social anthropologist dealing with living groups, ethnicity is largely a matter of self-identification and categorization by neighbouring others (see Barth 1969). The archaeologist without access to such direct testimony must generally resort to stylistic comparisons in order to assess the degree of "objective" cultural similarity. There is no direct evidence on the self-identification of the Franklin Bay people. However, we do know that their Avvaqmiut neighbours considered them to be Mackenzie Inuit "like themselves," and at the same time noted that they were territorially distinct, since they rarely travelled north and west of Iglulualuit, and then only to trade. Archaeologically, the Franklin Bay people were clearly Western Eskimo, and specifically resemble Mackenzie Inuit. There is thus no reason to doubt that they were Mackenzie Inuit, and represent a sixth territorial group, one which apparently disappeared early in the 19th century, as Stefansson's sources reported. We can refer to them as "Iglulualumiut" ("people of Iglulualuit"), after what

CHAPTER 9: CHRONOLOGY AND CULTURAL POSITION

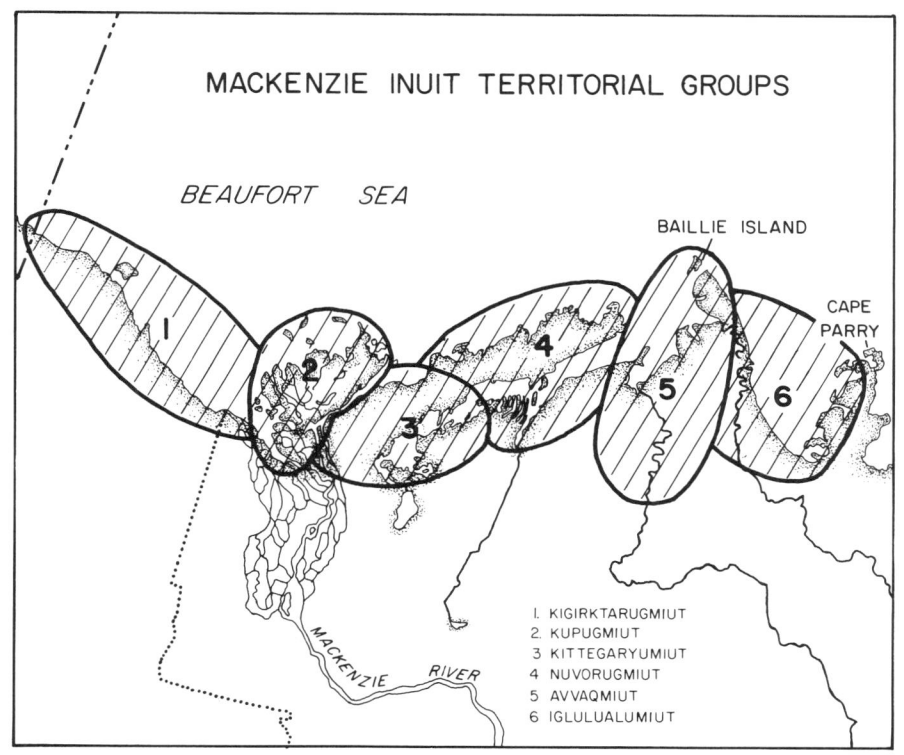

FIGURE 10

MACKENZIE INUIT TERRITORIAL GROUPS

appears to have been their largest village. Other, better-known Mackenzie Inuit groups were similarly named (Kittegarymiut, Nuvorugmiut, Avvaqmiut, etc.).

Stylistic variability between Mackenzie Inuit territorial groups is poorly understood, since only a single large site collection has been previously published. This is the Kittigazuit

IGLULUALUMIUT PREHISTORY

assemblage (McGhee 1974), and it represents the Kittegaryumiut, of the East Channel of the Mackenzie River. The Pt. Atkinson collection from Nuvurak (Mathiassen 1930) and the Kugaluk site (Morrison 1988a) both suggest that the Nuvorugmiut of the Tuktoyaktuk Peninsula area were stylistically very similar to the Kittegaryumiut, while small Avvaqmiut collections from the Barry site (Morrison 1988b) and several localities on the Cape Bathurst Peninsula (Wissler, 1916; LeBlanc 1987) are also very typical. By contrast, the Iglulualumiut do show some stylistic differences with other Mackenzie Inuit, such as the apparent absence from Iglulualumiut sites of fish-hook shanks with separate stone sinkers (see Mathiassen 1930: 12; McGhee 1974: 54), of straight bone fish-hooks with notched ends (see Morrison 1988a: Pl. 2, m-q), and of arrowheads made on caribou metapodial blanks (see Morrison 1988a: 40-41). The Iglulualumiut, in turn, appear to have had a propensity for bird bunts with smooth rather than lobed faces, and employed a type of small flat lance head more characteristic of the Eastern Arctic. These traits are comparatively minor, and will probably decrease in number as more sites are excavated.

More compelling is the absence from Iglulualumiut sites of the net floats, sinkers, and gauges so common from Mackenzie Inuit sites further west. This absence agrees with Stefansson's observations on the Langton Bay and Okat collections, and with his ethnographic information (Stefansson 1913: 332; 1914a: 332). Testimony on the use of seal nets at Iglulualuit suggests that economic and perhaps environmental factors may have been the major limiting factors, rather than the mere knowledge of netting techniques. Panigyuk, Stefansson's informant, recalled that the Iglulualumiut knew of the use of fish nets further west, but did not use them themselves. But this neglect of fish netting, nonetheless, is a major characteristic distinguishing the Iglulualumiut from their western neighbours.

CHAPTER 10

IGLULUALUMIUT PREHISTORY

Iglulualumiut Origins

At some time in the early fifteenth century, the Thule culture occupation of Franklin Bay came to an end, to be replaced by the Iglulualumiut. This change is most clearly reflected in the switch from predominantly open to predominantly closed socket harpoon heads, and is similar to the change from Thule to Recent Eskimo culture described in most other areas of the New World Arctic (Giddings and Anderson 1986; Stanford 1976; McGhee 1972; McCartney 1977). In Franklin Bay, as elsewhere, a crucial question is the nature of the relationship between the Thule and Recent occupations. Did the Recent culture develop solely from a local Thule culture base, or is it the product of cultural fusion, migration and population replacement? In most areas, the present consensus favours *in situ* development. The major text on Mackenzie Inuit prehistory, however, presents a more complicated model (McGhee 1974).

McGhee proposed that Mackenzie Inuit origins lay partially in a pre-Thule occupation, "part of an older cultural pattern, perhaps of riverine-adapted peoples occupying the interior areas from the Bering Sea to the Mackenzie River. In the Mackenzie Delta, as in western Alaska, this pattern may not have been completely obliterated by the development and spread of Thule culture" (McGhee 1974: 93). He points to close similarities, particularly in fishing technology, between Mackenzie Inuit culture at Kittigazuit and "Arctic Woodland culture" sites on the Kobuk River of west Alaska, noting that these similarities were not shared with Thule and Recent material at Pt. Barrow, or with Eastern Arctic Thule. Included are fish-hook shanks and netting gear. Other, less obviously "adaptive" shared traits include cruciform houses, horned kayaks, upright harpoon finger-rests, chipped-stone lance points, stone saws, rectangularly sectioned bows, sleeve-type adze heads, and centre-hump grindstones (see

IGLULUALUMIUT PREHISTORY

McGhee 1974: 88-89).

    Recent research has not supported McGhee's model. The Arctic Woodland sequence has now been firmly grounded in Thule culture, without need of any reference to a pre-Thule, Norton or Ipiutak antecedent (Giddings and Anderson 1986). The Ipiutak occupation of interior north Alaska, in fact, has proved to have had essentially no impact on developing Inuit/Inupiat culture (Gerlach and Hall 1988), while none of McGhee's cross-ties between Mackenzie Inuit and Arctic Woodland culture can be shown to have an immediate origin outside of the Thule tradition. Like all other Inuktitut/Inupiat-speakers, both the Mackenzie Inuit and the Arctic Woodlanders share a general Thule culture origin, and any specific similarities must be interpreted in historic terms within that context. This is not to deny the importance of connections between the western Canadian Arctic and interior and west Alaska; indeed Clachan phase sites indicate that it was important even before the development of Mackenzie Inuit culture. At the same time, other Mackenzie Inuit traits point to the importance of ties with the Pt. Barrow area (for instance, Nunagiak barbed and Brower harpoon heads), and the Central Arctic (shouldered snow knives, copper, and the soapstone pots recorded historically).

    There are a number of mechanisms to account for continued similarities between Mackenzie Inuit and other regional societies, particularly west Alaskans. Population movement during times of environmental stress may have been a factor (see Amsden 1979: 406). However, trade was probably the main form of continued contact, as McGhee has stressed. There is some evidence that the beginnings of the complex trade system documented historically coincide with the Recent period (Hickey 1979), suggesting the possibility of some sort of causal relationship between complex institutional trade and the rise of specific regional societies in the Western Arctic. Certainly there is good evidence of trade in Recent Franklin Bay assemblages. Situated on the far eastern edge

CHAPTER 10: IGLULUALUMIUT PREHISTORY

of the Western Arctic, the Iglulualumiut would also have been on the far end of Beringian trade networks, and thus perhaps middlemen in the inter-regional trade with the Central Arctic (see Stefansson 1914b). In this light it is interesting to note the presence of tools in local assemblages which appear to be of direct Central Arctic origin, such as a fish-hook plug and several classic Copper Inuit-style men's knife handles.

Despite continued contacts outside the Amundsen Gulf area, there is considerable evidence that the Mackenzie Inuit in general, and the Iglulualumiut in particular, developed from a local Thule culture base. A number of artifact types and traits specific to the area support this notion of direct local continuity. Discussion centres largely on material from Franklin Bay, but of necessity reference must also be made to the Washout site, and previously-known Mackenzie Inuit sites such as Kittigazuit, Radio Creek, and Pt. Atkinson.

Harpoon Heads: Despite the general shift from open to closed sockets, there is excellent continuity between Clachan phase Thule and Mackenzie Inuit harpoon heads. The dominant Mackenzie Inuit type, Barrow/Nuwuk, occurs in most Clachan phase Thule collections, including Booth Island. Conversely, Thule type 2 and Clachan harpoon heads, which are very abundant in local Thule sites, appear also in the Langton Bay collection, and at Pt. Atkinson (Mathiassen 1930: Pl.1, figs. 1-2). Moreover, the single harpoon head from Radio Creek is also of Clachan open socket type (McGhee 1974: Pl. 23,a). Considered by McGhee (1974) as a very early Mackenzie Inuit site, Radio Creek might even be classified as transitional from Thule. Another specific link are rare, flat, double line-hole harpoon heads, ultimately of Eastern Arctic derivation. They appear in Clachan phase Thule sites (Booth Island and Jackson), and also in the early levels of Kittigazuit. Nunagiak barbed harpoon heads appear in both local Thule (Booth

IGLULUALUMIUT PREHISTORY

Island and Washout) and Mackenzie Inuit sites (Iglulualuit and Kittigazuit), while the closely similar Brower type is found at Langton Bay and Pt. Atkinson. A final trait linking Mackenzie Inuit and Thule harpoon heads are the sharp shoulder spurs seen on Clachan phase harpoon heads from Booth Island and Clachan, and on specimens from Langton Bay. Some of these are on "Thule type" harpoon heads, but a Brower harpoon head from Langton Bay is also equipped with such spurs. They seem to be unknown outside of the Amundsen-Coronation Gulf area.

Arrowheads: Again, antler arrowheads from Thule and Recent sites seriate well. Langton Bay, Radio Creek, and the lower levels of Kittigazuit have all produced arrowheads with "Thule" tang forms, particularly knobbed, conically-knobbed, and ringed tangs (McGhee 1974: Table 2, 78). More characteristic of Mackenzie Inuit arrowheads are spurred conical tangs, but they also occur in Clachan phase Thule assemblages (Booth Island, Clachan, etc.). Sharp shoulder spurs or points similar to those on harpoon heads occur also on the occasional arrowhead; again the trait seems to be unique to the area. Arrowheads with such spurs at found at both Booth Island and Langton Bay.

Bird Bunts: Smooth-faced bird bunts seem to be common only in the Amundsen Gulf area. They appear in all of the Franklin Bay sites, and are the only type occurring at Langton Bay and Okat, on one hand, and Booth Island, on the other.

Lance Heads: Small, flat, endbladed lance heads, like those used in the Eastern Arctic, are present in both Mackenzie Inuit (Langton Bay, Okat) and Thule (Booth Island) assemblages. Similar lance heads are absent from Alaska.

Fish-hook Shanks: Although their ultimate origin may be west Alaska, fish-hook shanks occur in late local Thule sites such as

CHAPTER 10: IGLULUALUMIUT PREHISTORY

Washout, Booth Island, and Jackson, as well as being an important Mackenzie Inuit trait.

Snow Knives: Single-shouldered snow knives apparently derived from the Eastern Arctic are the usual type employed by Mackenzie Inuit, appearing at sites like Radio Creek, Pt. Atkinson, Okat, Langton Bay, and probably Kittigazuit. They are identical to snow knives from Clachan phase Thule sites (Booth Island and Jackson), but quite different from the usual Alaskan form.

Miscellaneous: Several traits which McGhee (1974: Table 5) lists as specifically linking Mackenzie Inuit with west Alaskans have since been found in western Canadian Arctic Thule sites, although not specifically in the Franklin Bay area. Included are upright harpoon finger-rests, found at Clachan (Morrison 1983a: Pl. 9,a), birch-bark baskets, found at the nearby Beulah site (Morrison 1983a: Fig. 20), and beaver-tooth knives, found at Washout (Yorga 1980: 90).

The De-Population of Amundsen Gulf

The nature of events further east in Amundsen Gulf should be considered, since this area was also occupied by Clachan phase Thule people. Its de-population, whenever that event occurred, would have had a major effect on communication with the developing Copper Inuit, and on the development of the Iglulualumiut themselves. We know that the southern Amundsen Gulf coast was abandoned by at least the mid-19th century, but that Stefansson thought that it had been occupied by Mackenzie Inuit, or Mackenzie Inuit-like people, until that time (Stefansson 1914a: 11-12, 17, 25). As we have seen, his reasons for thinking so are probably flawed. Writing before the recognition of Thule culture, Stefansson understandably mistook Thule houses for those of the Mackenzie Inuit. Early historic indications of people in the area

IGLULUALUMIUT PREHISTORY

are very few, and can all be attributed to travelling or trading parties, rather than a resident population. An example would be Richardson's observation in 1826 of "recent footsteps of a small party of Eskimaux...seen on the beach," just west of the Croker River (in Franklin 1971: 246). Trading journeys between Copper and Mackenzie Inuit continued into the mid-nineteenth century, and early twentieth century accounts speak of Copper Inuit travelling all the way to Baillie Island to trade (Jenness 1922: 44). Yet having dispensed with Stefansson's suggestion, we are no further forward in proposing a model of occupation.

Any such model must be tentative in the extreme, given the dearth of archaeological work in the area. Yet it may be significant that the few collections from eastern Amundsen Gulf are all attributable to Clachan phase Thule, and not to Recent occupations. Included here are the Jackson, Vaughan, and Morris sites (Taylor 1972), and the Inman River site (ASC Collections). Until evidence to the contrary should appear, the simplest hypothesis is the abandonment of the area by about A.D. 1400 or 1450, at the end of the Thule period. Suggested reasons for this abandonment must be even more tentative. Stefansson (1914a: 25) speaks of a breakdown in trade relations, but this is more likely to have been a consequence than a cause of abandonment. A fifteenth-century abandonment does, however, coincide with the onset of a deteriorating climatic episode known as the Neo-Boreal period (Nichols 1975). Colder summer conditions, reflected in the palynological data, could have resulted in the build-up of multi-year ice, with disastrous effects on sea mammal populations. There is evidence that the Coronation Gulf area suffered a population crash, followed by major economic re-adjustment at this time (McGhee 1972; Morrison 1983a). The consequences in Amundsen Gulf may have been even more disastrous, but until excavation is undertaken this remains only a suggestion.

Whatever the cause of abandonment, at this stage of research

CHAPTER 10: IGLULUALUMIUT PREHISTORY

it is important simply to appreciate its effects. No longer was there an essentially unbroken chain of occupation along the entire Arctic coast of North America. A reduction in communication between the Western and Central Arctic helped to define both regions, by separating them from one another. Gaps in occupation may have had nearly as much to do with the development of distinct regional patterns of Eskimo culture, as did the economic adaptation to local environments which went with it. No longer were the Central and Western Canadian Arctic joined in a common cultural phase, regardless of probable local economic differences. By the historic period, and despite some continued trade, the Mackenzie and Copper Inuit were probably the most dissimilar neighbouring pair of Eskimo regional groups in the New World Arctic Arctic.

Most of the change, of course, occurred among the Copper Inuit, who lived in a harsh and limited environment not really suited to what Steensby (1917) has called a Neoeskimo way of life. It was they who dropped open-water hunting and "permanent" sod houses, while the Iglulualumiut, on the other side of a now-deserted Amundsen Gulf, continued to enjoy a socioeconomic pattern which was a development from, rather than an abandonment of, their Thule culture legacy.

It is difficult to estimate the Iglulualumiut population at its late prehistoric peak. Iglulualuit itself could have housed many hundreds of people; as many as 500 if the excavated houses are typical. This, however, assumes that all of the houses were occupied contemporaneously, which is unlikely. The other known villages, Okat and Langton Bay, seem to have contained from three to five houses each, which is typical of village size in most of the western Canadian Arctic (McGhee 1972: 54; Morrison 1988a; 1988b). Probably a total population of about 200-500 people is on the right order of magnitude; on the small side for a Mackenzie Inuit society. It is possible that by the early 19th century this

IGLULUALUMIUT PREHISTORY

number had already been significantly reduced. Iglulualuit seems to have been abandoned by at least the beginning of the 19th century, to judge by the absence of standing houses in 1826. It is also noteworthy that there is no clear archaeological evidence of a historic occupation even from Okat and Langton Bay, which we know from ethnographic sources were occupied, however tenuously, well into the nineteenth century.

The abandonment of the southern coast of Amundsen Gulf was completed before 1850, when Iglulualumiut society finally collapsed. Information depends upon a single informant, who was a young girl at the time. According to her, abandonment was the consequence of starvation and disease, probably within the period between 1835 and 1845. Starvation can be caused by purely local environmental and even social conditions, and is difficult to investigate without direct sources. On the other hand, a disease epidemic as early as 1835 or 1840 is surprising among Western Arctic Inuit, since there is no historical reference to significant disease prior to a measles epidemic in the mid-1860s (see Morrison 1988a: 8). However, Indian groups to the south had been ravaged much earlier. Hare Indian bands trading into Fort Good Hope, for instance, were ravaged by a "dreadful sickness...a contagious distemper" as early as 1825 (Krech 1978: 713). The Iglulualumiut must have been in some contact with the Hare, who hunted to within about 30 kilometres of the Franklin Bay coast along the upper Horton River (Stefansson 1914a: 217-218; 280). We also know that Hare Indians carried on a significant trade with eastern Mackenzie Inuit between the 1820s, when Fort Good Hope was established, and 1861, when their middleman role was undermined by the establishment of Fort Anderson (see Morrison 1988a: 6-7). They may have been the source of a Franklin Bay epidemic.

The beginnings of the historic period may have contributed even more directly to the demise of the Iglulualumiut. European trade goods (principally iron and blue beads) were available

CHAPTER 10: IGLULUALUMIUT PREHISTORY

around the mouth of the Mackenzie River at least as early as 1789 (Mackenzie 1970: 208), traded by Alaskan Inupiat intermediaries from Russian trading posts on the Bering Sea coast (see Franklin 1971: 130). It is possible that many Iglulualumiut moved west, particularly to Baillie Island, to gain access to these goods. The inducement would have been particularly strong if the Franklin Bay population were already ravaged by disease, or was for some other reason declining below a critical level. The timing of the abandonment of Franklin Bay between Richardson's first and second voyages strongly suggests that it is in some way a product of indirect European contact.

REFERENCES CITED

ASC. Old Catalogue and Collections of the Archaeological Survey of Canada, Canadian Museum of Civilization, Ottawa.

AMSDEN, CHARLES. 1979. Hard times: a case study from northern Alaska and implications for Arctic Prehistory. In, Thule Eskimo Culture: An Anthropological Retrospective, A. McCartney, ed., pp. 395-410. National Museum of Man, Mercury Series, Archaeological Survey of Canada Paper 88.

ARMSTRONG, ALEXANDER. 1857. A Personal Narrative of the Discovery of the North-West Passage. Hurst and Blackett: London.

ARNOLD, CHARLES. 1986. A nineteenth-century Mackenzie Inuit site near Inuvik, Northwest Territories. Arctic 39(1): 8-14.

ARNOLD, CHARLES AND CAROLE STIMMELL. 1983. An analysis of Thule pottery. Canadian Journal of Archaeology 7(1): 1-22.

BARTH, FREDRIK. 1969. Introduction to Ethnic Groups and Boundaries, F. Barth, ed., pp. 9-38. Little Brown: Boston.

CHIPMAN, KENNETH AND J. R. COX. 1924. Part B: Geographical notes on the Arctic coast of Canada. Report of the Canadian Arctic Expedition, 1914-19, 11: 1-42.
COLLINS, HENRY. 1937. Archaeology of St. Lawrence Island. Smithsonian Miscellaneous Collections, 96.

COLLINS, HENRY. 1952. Archaeological excavations at Resolute, Cornwallis Island, N.W.T. National Museum of Canada Bulletin, 126: 48-63.

DAVIS, ROLPH, KERWIN FINLEY AND JOHN RICHARDSON. 1980. The Present Status and Future Management of Arctic Marine Mammals in Canada. Report of the Science Advisory Board of the Northwest Territories, 3.

FORD, JAMES A. 1959. Eskimo Prehistory in the Vicinity of Pt. Barrow Alaska. Anthropological Papers of the American Museum of Natural History, 47(1).

FRANKLIN, JOHN. 1971. Narrative of a Second Expedition to the Shores of the Polar Sea in the Years 1825, 1826, and 1827. Hurtig: Edmonton.

GERLACH, S. CRAIG AND EDWIN HALL. 1988. The later prehistory of northern Alaska: the view from Tukuto Lake. In, The Late Prehistoric Development of Alaska's Native People, R. Shaw, R. Harritt and D. Dumond, eds., pp. 107-136. Alaska Anthropological Association Monograph Series, 4.

GIDDINGS, J. LOUIS. 1952. The Arctic Woodland Culture of the Kobuk River. University of Pennsylvania, University Museum Monograph, 8.

GIDDINGS, J. LOUIS. 1964. The Archaeology of Cape Denbigh. Brown University Press: Providence.

GIDDINGS, J. LOUIS AND DOUGLAS ANDERSON. 1986. Beach Ridge Archaeology of Cape Krusenstern. U.S. Department of the Interior, National Park Service, Publications in Archaeology, 20.

GORDON, BRYAN. 1988. Nadlok and its unusual antler dwellings. Arctic, 41(2): 160-161.

GRIFFIN, JAMES AND ROSCOE WILMETH. 1964. The ceramic complexes at Iyatayet. Appendix to: The Archaeology of Cape Denbigh, by J. Louis Giddings, pp. 271-303. Brown University Press: Providence.

HALL, EDWIN. 1971. Kangiguksuk: a cultural reconstruction of a sixteenth century Eskimo Site in northern Alaska. Arctic Anthropology, 8(1): 1-101.

HALL, EDWIN. 1981. Cultural resource site potential. In, Cultural Resources in the mid-Beaufort Sea Region, by David Libbey and Edwin Hall. North Slope Borough Coastal Zone Management Plan Report: Barrow Alaska.

HICKEY, CLIFFORD. 1979. The historic Beringian trade network: its nature and origins. In, Thule Eskimo Culture: An Anthropological Retrospective, A. McCartney, ed., pp. 411-434. National Museum of Man, Mercury Series, Archaeological Survey of Canada Paper 88.

JENNESS, DIAMOND. 1922. The Life of the Copper Eskimos. Report of the Canadian Arctic Expedition, 1913-18, 12(a).

JENNESS, DIAMOND. 1946. Material Culture of the Copper Eskimo. Report of the Canadian Arctic Expedition, 1913-18, 16.

KRECH, SHEPARD. 1978. Disease, starvation, and Northern Athapaskan social organization. American Ethnologist, 5(4): 710-732.

LEBLANC, RAYMOND. 1987. Report of Activities - NOGAP 1986: northern Yukon to Cape Bathurst Peninsula. MS 2834, on file with the Archaeological Survey of Canada, Canadian Museum of Civilization, Ottawa.

LE MOUEL, JEAN-FRANCOIS AND MARYKE LE MOUEL. 1987. <u>OdPp-2 - Coop Site: Preliminary Report on the 1986 Summer Campaign.</u> Museum National d'Histoire Naturelle: Paris.

LE MOUEL, MARYKE. Personal communication, September, 1988, Canadian Museum of Civilization, Ottawa.

MACKAY, J. ROSS. 1958. <u>The Anderson River Map-Area, N.W.T.</u> Mines and Technical Surveys, Geographical Bramch, Memoir 5.

MACKAY, J. ROSS. 1981. Dating the Horton River breakthrough, District of Mackenzie. <u>Geological Survey of Canada Paper</u>, 81-1B: 129-132.

MACFARLANE, RODERICK. 1905. Notes on mammals collected and observed in the northern Mackenzie River District, Northwest Territories of Canada. <u>Proceedings of the U.S. National Museum</u>, 28: 673-764.

MACKENZIE, ALEXANDER. 1970. <u>The Journals and Letters of Sir Alexander Mackenzie</u>, W. Kaye Lamb, ed. Macmillan: Toronto.

MACNEISH, RICHARD. 1956. Archaeological reconnaissance of the delta of the Mackenzie River and Yukon Coast. <u>National Museum of Canada Bulletin,</u> 142: 46-81.

MANNING, THOMAS. 1956. Narrative of a second Defense Research Board expedition to Banks Island. <u>Arctic</u>, 9(1-2).

MASON, OTIS. 1902. Aboriginal American harpoons. <u>Annual Report of the U.S. National Museum for 1900</u>, pp. 189-304.

MATHIASSEN, THERKEL. 1927a. Archaeology of the Central Eskimos I: descriptive part. Report of the Fifth Thule Expedition 1921-24, 4(1).

MATHIASSEN, THERKEL. 1927b. Archaeology of the Central Eskimos II: analytical part. Report of the Fifth Thule Expedition 1921-24, 4(2).

MATHIASSEN, THERKEL. 1930. Archaeological Collections from the Western Eskimos. Report of the Fifth Thule Expedition 1921-24, 10(1).

MCCARTNEY, ALLEN. 1977. Thule Eskimo Prehistory along Northwestern Hudson Bau. National Museum of Man, Mercury Series, Archaeological Survey of Canada Paper 70.

MCCULLOUGH, KAREN. 1986. The Ruin Island Phase of Thule Culture in the Eastern High Arctic. Unpublished doctoral dissertation, Department of Anthropology, University of Toronto.

MCGHEE, ROBERT. 1969/70. Speculations on climatic change and Thule culture development. Folk, 11-12: 172-184.

MCGHEE, ROBERT. 1972. Copper Eskimo Prehistory. National Museum of Man, Publications in Archaeology, 2.

MCGHEE, ROBERT. 1974. Beluga Hunters: an archaeological reconstruction of the history and culture of the Mackenzie Delta Kittegaryumiut. Memorial University of Newfoundland, Newfoundland Social and Economic Studies, 13.

MCGHEE, ROBERT. 1984a. The Thule Village at Brooman Point, High Arctic Canada. National Museum of Man, Mercury Series, Archaeological Survey of Canada Paper 125.

MCGHEE, ROBERT. 1984b. Thule prehistory of Canada. In, Handbook of North American Indians, Vol. 5, Arctic, D. Damas ed., pp. 369-376. Smithsonian Institution: Washington.

MCGHEE, ROBERT. 1984c. The timing of the Thule migration. Polarforschung, 54(1): 1-7.

MCGHEE, ROBERT. 1988. A scenario for Eskimo-Aleut prehistory. In, The Late Prehistoric Development of Alaska's Native People, R. Shaw, R. Harritt and D. Dumond, eds., pp. 369-378. Alaska Anthropological Association Monograph Series, 4.

MCKINLAY, WILLIAM. 1976. Karluk: The Great Untold Story of Arctic Exploration. Butler and Tanner: London.
M'CLURE, ROBERT. 1969. The Discovery of the North-West Passage. Hurtig: Edmonton.

MIERTSCHING, JOHANN. 1967. Frozen Ships: The Arctic Diary of Johann Miertsching, L. Neatby, trans. Macmillan: Toronto.

MORRISON, DAVID. 1981. A preliminary statement on Neo-Eskimo occupations in western Coronation Gulf, NWT. Arctic, 34(3): 261-269.

MORRISON, DAVID. 1983a. Thule Culture in Western Coronation Gulf, N.W.T. National Museum of Man, Mercury Series, Archaeological Survey of Canada Paper 116.

MORRISON, DAVID. 1983b. Thule sea mammal hunting in the western central Arctic. Arctic Anthropology, 20(2): 61-78.

MORRISON, DAVID. 1987. Thule and historic copper use in the Copper Inuit area. American Antiquity, 52(1): 3-12.

MORRISON, DAVID. 1988a. *The Kugaluk Site and the Nuvorugmiut*. Canadian Museum of Civilization, Mercury Series, Archaeological Survey of Canada Paper 137.

MORRISON, DAVID. 1988b. Report on Barry site excavations, 1988. MS on file with the Archaeological Survey of Canada, Canadian Museum of Civilization, Ottawa.

MURDOCH, JOHN. 1892. *Ethnological Results of the Point Barrow Expedition*. Ninth Annual Report of the Bureau of American Ethnology.

NICHOLS, HARVEY. 1975. *Palynological and Paleoclimatic Study of the Late Quaternary Displacement of the Boreal Forest-Tundra Ecotone in Keewatin and Mackenzie, N.W.T., Canada*. Institute of Arctic and Alpine Research, Occasional Paper 15.

NULIGAK. 1966. *I, Nuligak*, M. Metayer, trans. Peter Martin: Toronto.

PETITOT, EMILE. 1970. *The Amerindians of the Canadian Northwest in the 19th Century, Vol. 1: The Tchiglit Eskimos*, D. Savoie, ed. Mackenzie Delta Research Project, 9.

PULLEN, H. F. 1979. *The Pullen Expedition*. Arctic History Press: Toronto.

RICHARDSON, JOHN. 1851. *Arctic Searching Expedition*, Vol. 1 Longmans, Brown, Green, and Longmans: London.

STANFORD, DENNIS. 1976. *The Walakpa Site, Alaska*. Smithsonian Contributions to Anthropology, 20.

STEENSBY, HANS. 1917. *An Anthropogeographical Study of the Origin of the Eskimo Culture*. Meddelelser om Gronland, 53(2).

STEFANSSON, VIHLJALMUR. 1913. *My Life with the Eskimo*. Macmillan: New York.

STEFANSSON, VIHLJALMUR. 1914a. *The Stefansson-Anderson Arctic Expedition: Preliminary Ethnological Results*. Anthropological Papers of the American Museum of Natural History, 14(1).

STEFANSSON, VIHLJALMUR. 1914b. *Prehistoric and Present Commerce among the Arctic Coast Eskimo*. Geological Survey of Canada, Museum Bulletin, 6.

STEFANSSON, VIHLJALMUR. 1921. *The Friendly Arctic*. Macmillan: New York.

STOMBERG, RICHARD. 1987. Cache Point (NhTs-2) and Mackenzie Inuit prehistory. Paper presented to the Annual Meetings of the Society for American Archaeology, Toronto.

TAYLOR, J. GARTH. 1974. *Netsilik Eskimo Material Culture*. Universitetsforlaget: Oslo.

TAYLOR, WILLIAM E., Jr. 1963. Hypotheses on the origin of Canadian Thule culture. *American Antiquity*, 28(4): 456-464.

TAYLOR, WILLIAM E., Jr. 1972. *An Archaeological Survey between Cape Parry and Cambridge Bay, N.W.T., Canada in 1963*. National Museum of Man, Mercury Series, Archaeological Survey of Canada Paper, 1.

USHER, PETER. 1971. *Fur Trade Posts of the Northwest Territories 1870-1970*. Northern Science Research Group 71-4.

WILMETH, ROSCOE. 1978. *Canadian Archaeological Radiocarbon Dates (Revised Version)*. National Museum of Man, Mercury Series, Archaeological Survey of Canada Paper 77.

WISSLER, CLARK. 1916. *Harpoons and Darts in the Stefansson Collection*. Anthropological Papers of the American Museum of Natural History, 14(2).

YORGA, BRIAN. 1980. *Washout: A Western Thule Site on Herschel Island, Yukon Territory*. National Museum of Man, Mercury Series, Archaeological Survey of Canada Paper 98.

PLATES

A Note on Catalogue Numbers: Catalogue numbers prefixed with the code "NlRu-1" (the Borden Number of the Iglulualuit site) are part of the collections of the Archaeological Survey of Canada, Canadian Museum of Civilization (New Catalogue System), while those prefixed "IX.D" belong to the same institution, but filed under the Old Catalogue System. The prefix "60.1" refers to artifacts from the American Museum of Natural History. In all cases, numbers are transcribed as they appear on the artifact.

PLATE 1: IGLULUALUIT SEA HUNTING GEAR

FIGURE	DESCRIPTION AND CATALOGUE NUMBER	PAGE REFERENCE
a	harpoon head: NlRu-1-26	32
b	harpoon head: NlRu-1-97	32
c	harpoon head: NlRu-1-55	32
d	harpoon head: NlRu-1-212	32
e	harpoon head: 60.1-3148	32
f	dart head: NlRu-1-419	32
g	harpoon head: NlRu-1-423	32
h	harpoon head: NlRu-1-113	32
i	harpoon head blank: NlRu-1-10	32
j	harpoon endblade: NlRu-1-65	33
k	harpoon endblade: NlRu-1-313	33
l	harpoon endblade: NlRu-1-181	33
m	harpoon endblade: NlRu-1-454	33
n	harpoon endblade: NlRu-1-385	33

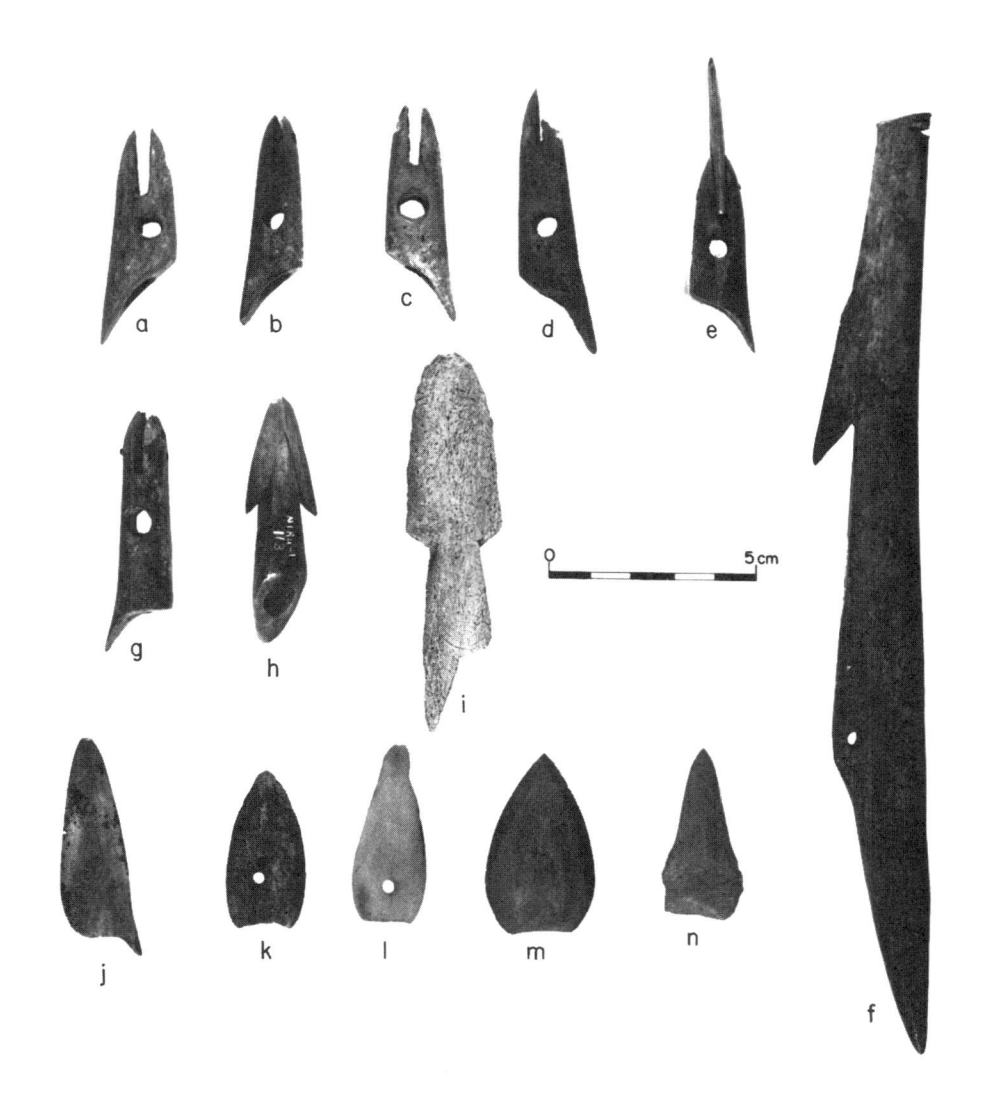

PLATE 1: IGLULUALUIT SEA HUNTING GEAR

PLATE 2: LANGTON BAY SEA HUNTING GEAR

FIGURE	DESCRIPTION AND CATALOGUE NUMBER	PAGE REFERENCE
a	harpoon head: 60.1-3315	34
b	harpoon head: 60.1-3334	34
c	harpoon head: 60.1-3315	34
d	harpoon head: 60.1-3315	34
e	harpoon head: 60.1-3315	34
f	harpoon head: 60.1-3333	34
g	harpoon head: 60.1-3315	34
h	harpoon head: 60.1-3315	34
i	harpoon head: 60.1-3315	34
j	harpoon head: 60.1-3332	34
k	harpoon head: 60.1-3315	34
l	harpoon head: 60.1-3339	34
m	harpoon head: 60.1-3315A	34
n	harpoon head: 60.1-3315A	34
o	harpoon head: 60.1-3315	34
p	harpoon endblade: 60.1-3335	35
q	lance head: 60.1-3315	36

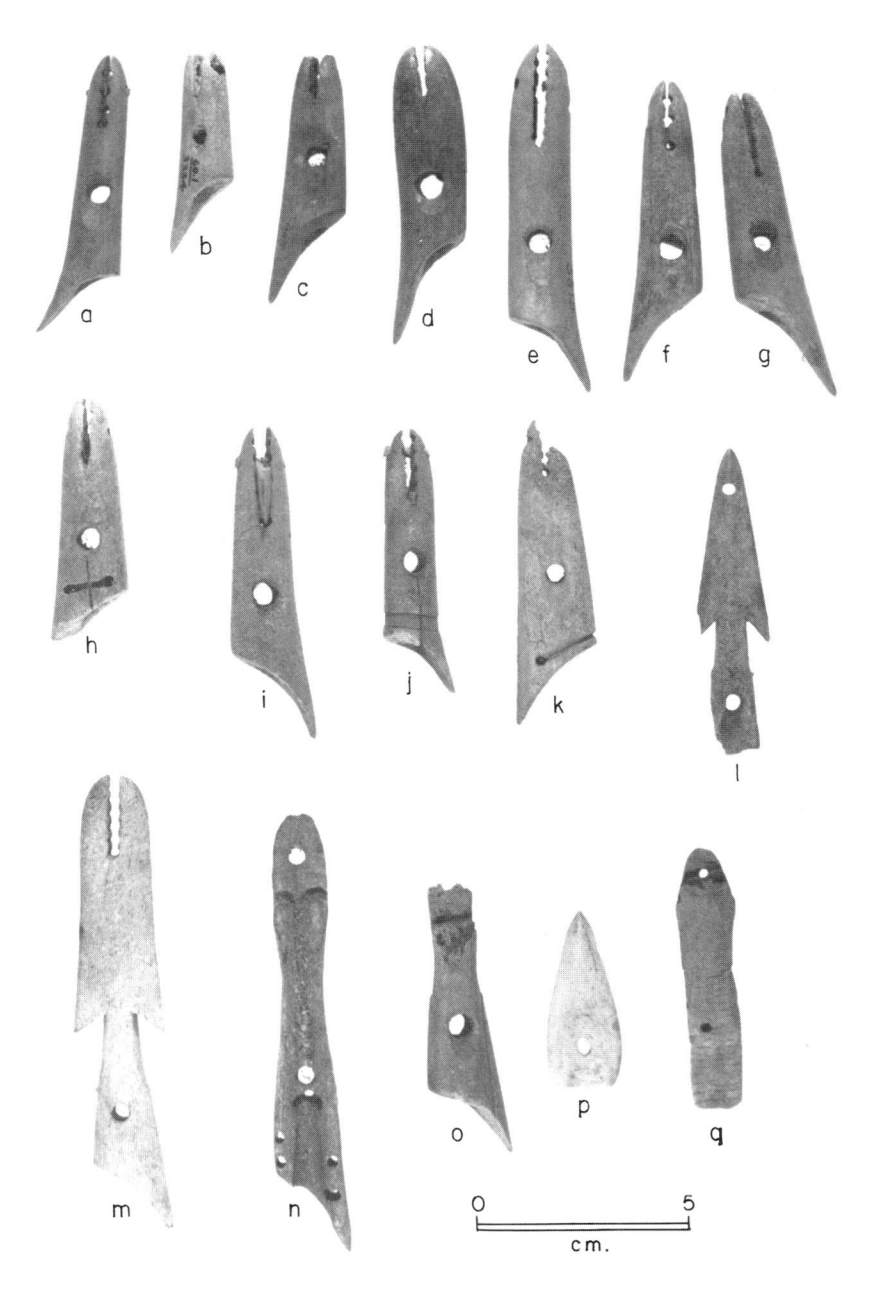

PLATE 2: LANGTON BAY SEA HUNTING GEAR

PLATE 3: LANGTON BAY SEA HUNTING GEAR

FIGURE	DESCRIPTION AND CATALOGUE NUMBER	PAGE REFERENCE
a	harpoon foreshaft: 60.1-3347	35
b	harpoon foreshaft: 60.1-3305	35
c	harpoon foreshaft: 60.1-3322	35
d	harpoon socketpiece: 60.1-3213	36
e	harpoon socketpiece: 60.1-3302	36

PLATE 3: LANGTON BAY SEA HUNTING GEAR

PLATE 4: OKAT SEA HUNTING GEAR

FIGURE	DESCRIPTION AND CATALOGUE NUMBER	PAGE REFERENCE
a	dart head: 60.1-3099	37
b	harpoon head: 60.1-3095	37
c	harpoon head: 60.1-3093	37
d	lance head: 60.1-3008	38
e	lance head: 60.1-3094	38
f	lance head: 60.1-3002	38
g	harpoon foreshaft: 60.1-2960	38
h	harpoon endblade: IX.D-62	37
i	harpoon socketpiece: 60.1-2966	38
j	harpoon (?) socketpiece: 60.1-2961	38
k	harpoon foreshaft: 60.1-3105	38
l	toggle: 60.1-3007	38

PLATE 4: OKAT SEA HUNTING GEAR

137

PLATE 5: BOOTH ISLAND SEA HUNTING GEAR

FIGURE	DESCRIPTION AND CATALOGUE NUMBER	PAGE REFERENCE
a	harpoon head: IX.D-261d	39
b	harpoon head: IX.D-261v	39
c	harpoon head: IX.D-261a	39
d	harpoon head: IX.D-261m	39
e	harpoon head: IX.D-261w	39
f	harpoon head: IX.D-261r	39
g	harpoon head: IX.D-261n	39
h	harpoon head: IX.D-261q	39
i	harpoon head: IX.D-265	39
j	harpoon head: IX.D-261z	39
k	harpoon head: IX.D-260s	39
l	harpoon head: IX.D-260x	39
m	harpoon head: IX.D-260a	39
n	harpoon head: IX.D-260v	39
o	harpoon head: IX.D-260h	39
p	harpoon head: IX.D-260g	39
q	harpoon head: IX.D-260q	39

PLATE 5: BOOTH ISLAND SEA MAMMAL HUNTING GEAR

PLATE 6: BOOTH ISLAND SEA HUNTING GEAR

FIGURE	DESCRIPTION AND CATALOGUE NUMBER	PAGE REFERENCE
a	harpoon head: IX.D-259f	39
b	harpoon head: IX.D-259b	39
c	harpoon head: IX.D-259c	39
d	harpoon head: IX.D-259i	39
e	harpoon head: IX.D-259a	39
f	harpoon head: IX.D-259h	39
g	harpoon head: IX.D-266	39
h	harpoon head: IX.D-267	39
i	harpoon head: IX.D-262c	39
j	harpoon head: IX.D-262d	39
k	harpoon head: IX.D-262a	39
l	harpoon head: IX.D-262b	39
m	harpoon endblade: IX.D-285h	41
n	harpoon endblade: IX.D-285l	41
o	lance head: IX.D-281j	42

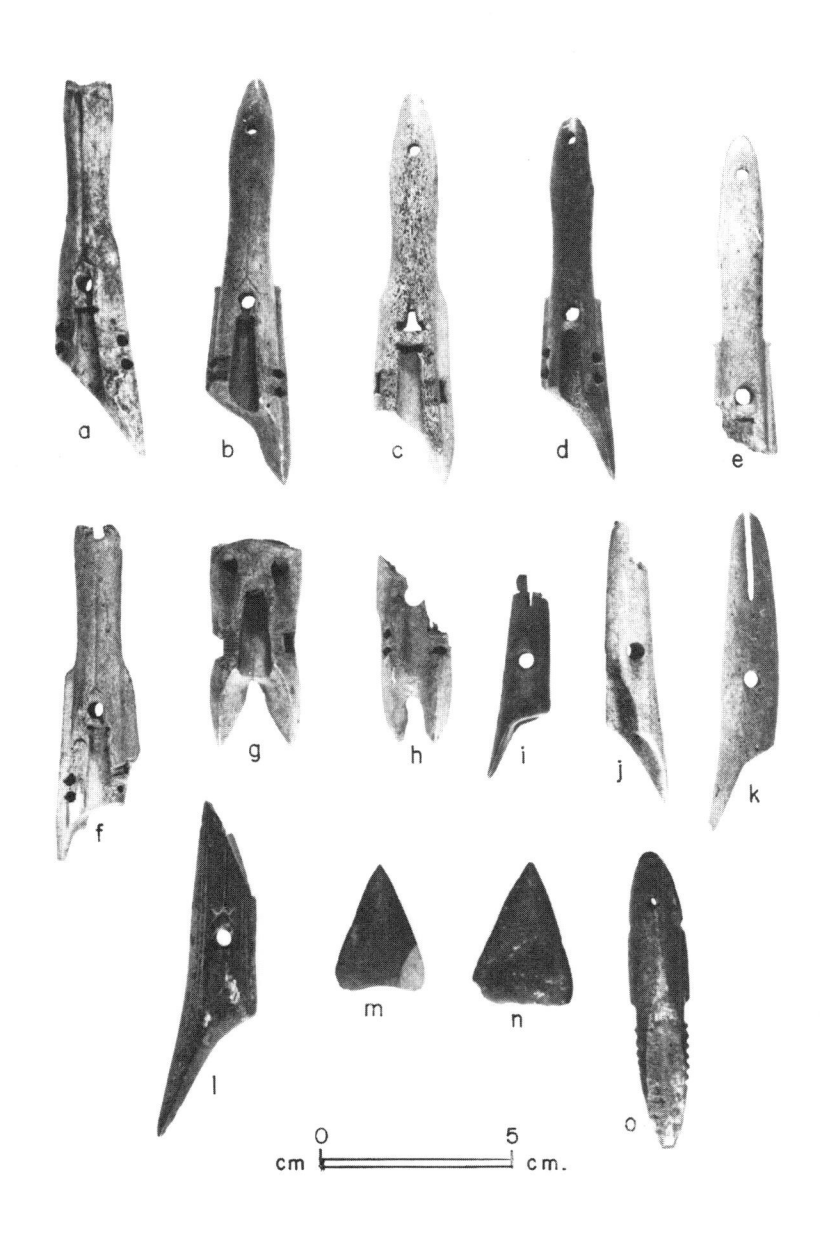

PLATE 6: BOOTH ISLAND SEA MAMMAL HUNTING GEAR

141

PLATE 7: BOOTH ISLAND SEA HUNTING GEAR

FIGURE	DESCRIPTION AND CATALOGUE NUMBER	PAGE REFERENCE
a	harpoon foreshaft: IX.D-251	41
b	harpoon foreshaft: IX.D-257	41
c	harpoon socketpiece: IX.D-249	41
d	seal indicator (?): IX.D-299r	42
e	dart head: IX.D-353	41
f	wound pin: IX.D-220	42
g	wound pin: IX.D-219	42
h	wound pin: IX.D-218	42
i	wound pin: IX.D-221	42
j	toggle: IX.D-359	42

PLATE 7: BOOTH ISLAND SEA HUNTING GEAR

143

PLATE 8: IGLULUALUIT LAND HUNTING GEAR

FIGURE	DESCRIPTION AND CATALOGUE NUMBER	PAGE REFERENCE
a	arrow point: NlRu-1-430	49
b	arrow point: NlRu-1-296	49
c	arrow point: NlRu-1-450	49
d	arrow point: NlRu-1-405	49
e	arrow point: NlRu-1-347	49
f	arrow point: NlRu-1-218	49
g	arrow point: NlRu-1-431	49
h	arrow point: NlRu-1-185	49
i	arrowhead: NlRu-1-416	48
j	arrowhead: 60.1-3145	48
k	arrowhead: NlRu-1-427	48
l	arrowhead: NlRu-1-425	48
m	arrowhead: NlRu-1-426	48
n	arrowhead: NlRu-1-175	48
o	archer's wrist guard: NlRu-1-57	49

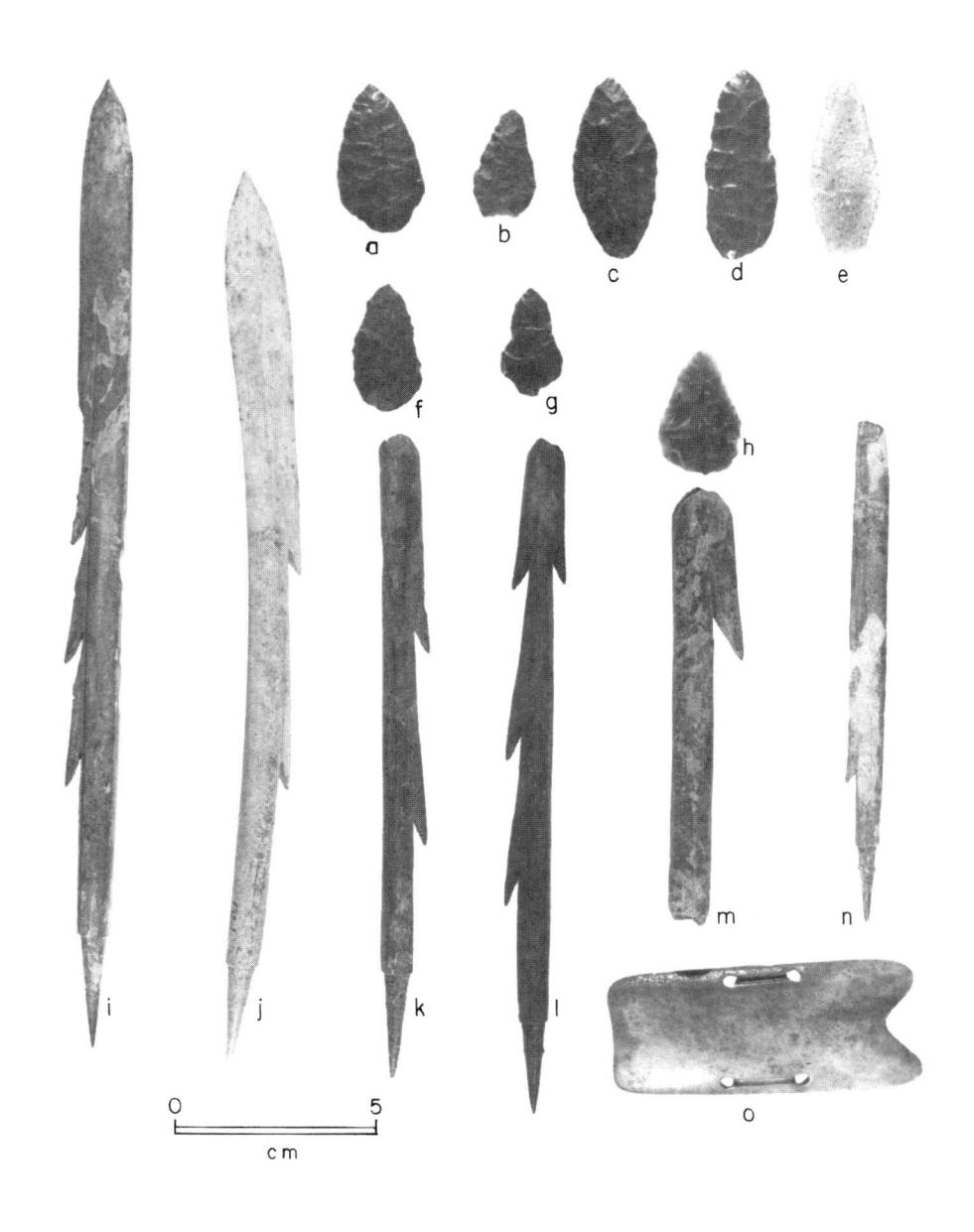

PLATE 8: IGLULUALUIT LAND HUNTING GEAR

145

PLATE 9: IGLULUALUIT LAND HUNTING GEAR

FIGURE	DESCRIPTION AND CATALOGUE NUMBER	PAGE REFERENCE
a	marlin spike: NlRu-1-376	49
b	arrowhead: NlRu-1-467	48
c	spear point: NlRu-1-342	49
d	spear point: NlRu-1-384	49
e	bird bunt: NlRu-1-95	49
f	bird bunt: NlRu-1-200	49
g	bird bunt: NlRu-1-207	49
h	spear point: NlRu-1-228	49
i	spear point: NlRu-1-386	49
j	spear point: NlRu-1-458	49
k	spear point: NlRu-1-353	49

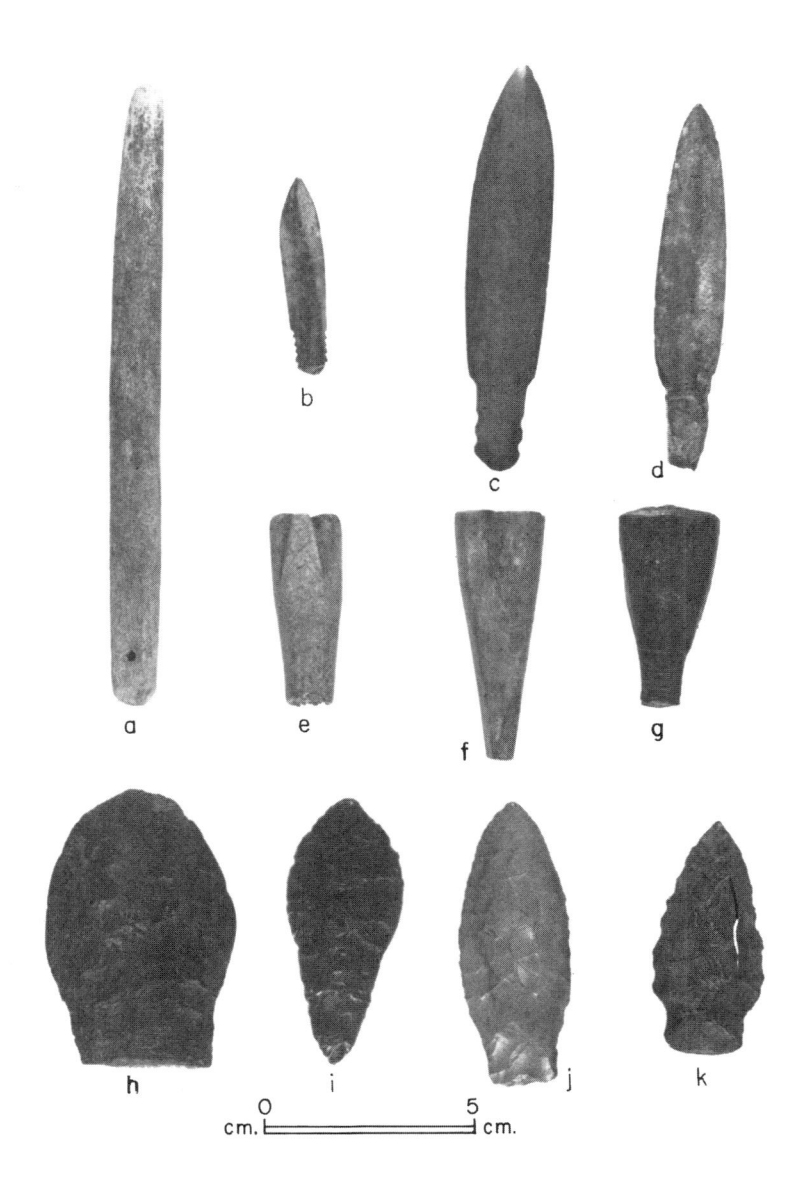

PLATE 9: IGLULUALUIT LAND HUNTING GEAR

PLATE 10: LANGTON BAY LAND HUNTING GEAR

FIGURE	DESCRIPTION AND CATALOGUE NUMBER	PAGE REFERENCE
a	arrowhead: 60.1-3317	50
b	arrowhead: 60.1-3317	50
c	arrowhead: 60.1-3317	50
d	arrowhead: 60.1-3317	50
e	arrowhead: 60.1-3315A	50
f	arrowhead: 60.1-3317	50
g	arrowhead: 60.1-3319	50
h	arrowhead: 60.1-3317	50
i	arrowhead: 60.1-3317	50
j	arrowhead: 60.1-3319	50
k	arrowhead: 60.1-3315B	50

PLATE 10: LANGTON BAY LAND HUNTING GEAR

149

PLATE 11: LANGTON BAY LAND HUNTING GEAR

FIGURE	DESCRIPTION AND CATALOGUE NUMBER	PAGE REFERENCE
a	arrowhead: 60.1-3338	50
b	arrowhead: 60.1-3319	50
c	arrow featherer: 60.1-3406	51
d	arrow featherer: 60.1-3407	51
e	bow wedge: 60.1-3339	51
f	bird bunt: 60.1-3313	51
g	bird bunt: 60.1-3312	51
h	bird bunt: 60.1-3324	51
i	bird bunt: 60.1-3314	51
j	bone dagger: 60.1-3309	51

PLATE 11: LANGTON BAY LAND HUNTING GEAR

PLATE 12: OKAT LAND HUNTING GEAR

FIGURE	DESCRIPTION AND CATALOGUE NUMBER	PAGE REFERENCE
a	arrowhead: 60.1-3027	52
b	arrowhead: 60.1-3000	52
c	arrowhead: 60.1-3098	52
d	arrowhead: 60.1-3374	52
e	arrow point: IX.D-16	52
f	arrow point: IX.D-17	52
g	arrow point: IX.D-21	52
h	arrow point: IX.D-15	52
i	arrow point: IX.D-12	52
j	arrow point: IX.D-20	52
k	arrow point: IX.D-14	52
l	arrow point: IX.D-18	52
m	arrow point: IX.D-13	52
n	sinew twister: 60.1-3024	52
o	shaft straightener: 60.1-3366	52

PLATE 12: OKAT LAND HUNTING GEAR

153

PLATE 13: BOOTH ISLAND LAND HUNTING GEAR

FIGURE	DESCRIPTION AND CATALOGUE NUMBER	PAGE REFERENCE
a	arrowhead: IX.D-281b	52
b	arrowhead: IX.D-281v	52
c	arrowhead: IX.D-281e	52
d	arrowhead: IX.D-281aa	52
e	arrowhead: IX.D-281h	52
f	arrowhead: IX.D-281k	52
g	arrowhead: IX.D-281z	52
h	arrowhead: IX.D-281q	52
i	arrowhead: IX.D-281ee	52
j	arrowhead: IX.D-281kk	52
k	arrow point: IX.D-281c	53
l	arrow point: IX.D-282a	53
m	bird bunt: IX.D-381	53
n	sinew twister: IX.D-314	53

PLATE 13: BOOTH ISLAND LAND HUNTING GEAR

PLATE 14: IGLULUALUIT FISHING GEAR

FIGURE	DESCRIPTION AND CATALOGUE NUMBER	PAGE REFERENCE
a	fish hook shank: NlRu-1-400	57
b	fish hook shank: NlRu-1-12	57
c	fish hook shank: NlRu-1-202	57
d	fish hook shank and barb: NlRu-1-249	57
e	fish hook barb: NlRu-1-186	57
f	fish spear prong: NlRu-1-248	57
g	fish spear prong: NlRu-1-403	57
h	fish spear prong: NlRu-1-369	57
i	fish spear prong: NlRu-1-199	57
j	fish spear prong: NlRu-1-440	57
k	fish spear prong: NlRu-1-49	57

PLATE 14: IGLULUALUIT FISHING GEAR

157

PLATE 15: LANGTON BAY FISHING GEAR

FIGURE	DESCRIPTION AND CATALOGUE NUMBER	PAGE REFERENCE
a	fish hook shank: 60.1-3342	58
b	fish hook shank: 60.1-3342	58
c	fish hook shank: 60.1-3342	58
d	fish hook shank: 60.1-3342	58
e	fish hook shank: 60.1-3342	58
f	fish hook shank: 60.1-3342	58
g	fish hook shank: 60.1-3339	58
h	fish hook shank: 60.1-3339	58
i	fish hook shank: 60.1-3327	58
j	fish hook shank: 60.1-3328	58
k	fish hook barb: 60.1-3342	59
l	fish hook barb: 60.1-3329	59
m	fish hook barb: 60.1-3342	59
n	fish hook barb: 60.1-3342	59
o	fish hook barb: 60.1-3407	59
p	trident centre prong: 60.1-3323	60
q-r	fish spear prongs: 60.1-3338, -3338	59
s-t	fish spear prongs: 60.1-3319, -3317a	59
u-w	trident barbs: 60.1-3330, -3342, -3406	59
x-y	trident barbs: 60.1-3324, -3342	59
z	fish lure: 60.1-3344	59
aa	fish lure (spoon): 60.1-3331	59
bb	ice pick: 60.1-3348	60

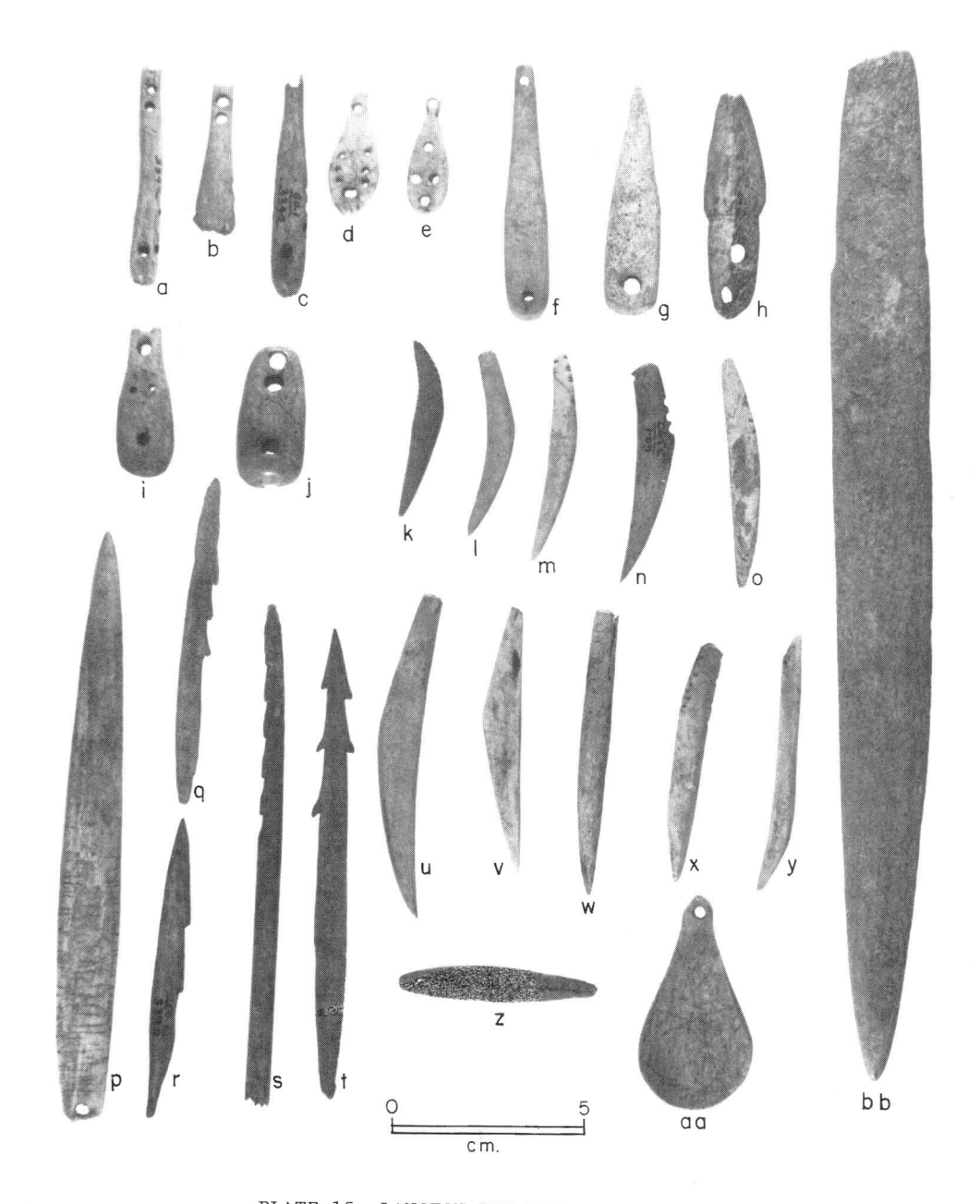

PLATE 15: LANGTON BAY FISHING GEAR

PLATE 16: OKAT AND BOOTH ISLAND FISHING GEAR

FIGURE	DESCRIPTION AND CATALOGUE NUMBER	PAGE REFERENCE
a	fish spear prong: 60.1-3097 (Okat)	60
b	fish spear prong: 60.1-2999 (Okat)	60
c	fish spear prong: 60.1-2984 (Okat)	60
d	fish spear prong: 60.1-3096 (Okat)	60
e	ice scoop: 60.1-3017 (Okat)	60
f	ice scoop fragment: IX.D-118 (Okat)	60
g	fish lure: IX.D-319 (Booth Is.)	61
h	fish lure: IX.D-356 (Booth Is.)	61
i	fish lure: IX.D-247 (Booth Is.)	61
j	ice pick: 60.1-2948 (Okat)	60
k	ice pick: 60.1-2947 (Okat)	60
l	fish hook shank: IX.D-232 (Booth Is.)	61
m	fish hook shank: IX.D-231 (Booth Is.)	61
n	fish hook shank: IX.D-233 (Booth Is.)	61

PLATE 16: OKAT AND BOOTH ISLAND FISHING GEAR

161

PLATE 17: IGLULUALUIT MEN'S TOOLS

FIGURE	DESCRIPTION AND CATALOGUE NUMBER	PAGE REFERENCE
a	fox-tooth graver: NlRu-1-452	70
b	endblade knife handle: NlRu-1-201	70
c	knife with copper blade: NlRu-1-70	70
d	knife handle fragment: NlRu-1-128	70
e	flint flaker: NlRu-1-339	71
f	drill socket (?): NlRu-1-471	72
g	drill socket (?): NlRu-1-406	72
h	drill socket (?): NlRu-1-325	72
i	slate knife endblade: NlRu-1-410	70
j	slate knife endblade: NlRu-1-324	70
k	slate knife endblade: NlRu-1-94	70
l	slate knife endblade: NlRu-1-283	70
m	slate knife endblade: NlRu-1-435	70
n	slate knife endblade: NlRu-1-191	70

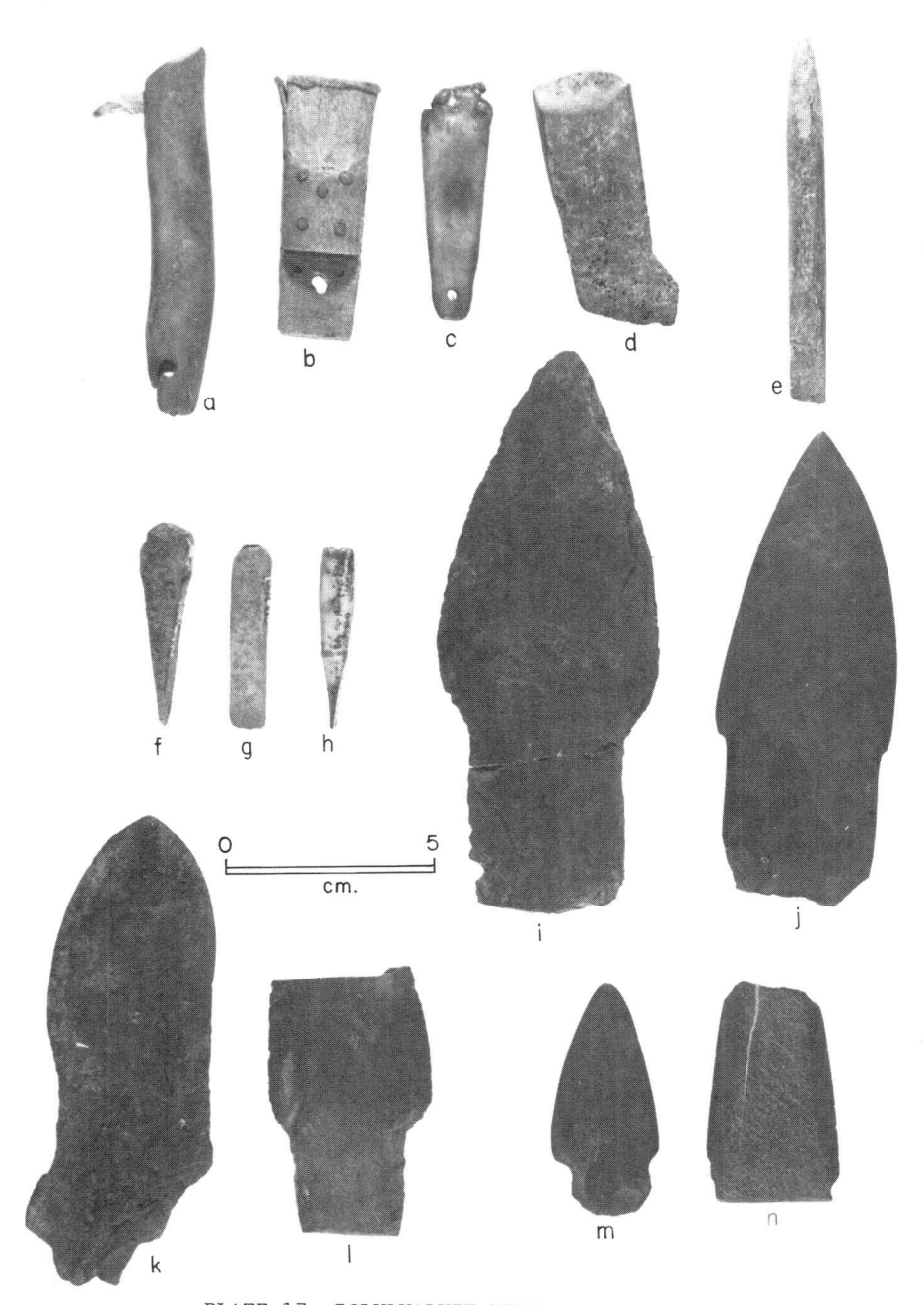

PLATE 17: IGLULUALUIT MEN'S TOOLS

PLATE 18: IGLULUALUIT MEN'S TOOLS AND TRANSPORTATION ITEMS

FIGURE	DESCRIPTION AND CATALOGUE NUMBER	PAGE REFERENCE
a	mattock: NlRu-1-462	72
b	wedge: NlRu-1-24	72
c	sawed slate: NlRu-1-397	-
d	sawed slate: NlRu-1-393	-
e	wedge: NlRu-1-221	72
f	sled shoe fragment: NlRu-1-13	66
g	snow shoe needle (?): NlRu-1-187	66
h	sled shoe fragment: NlRu-1-138	66
i	snow probe section: NlRu-1-211	66

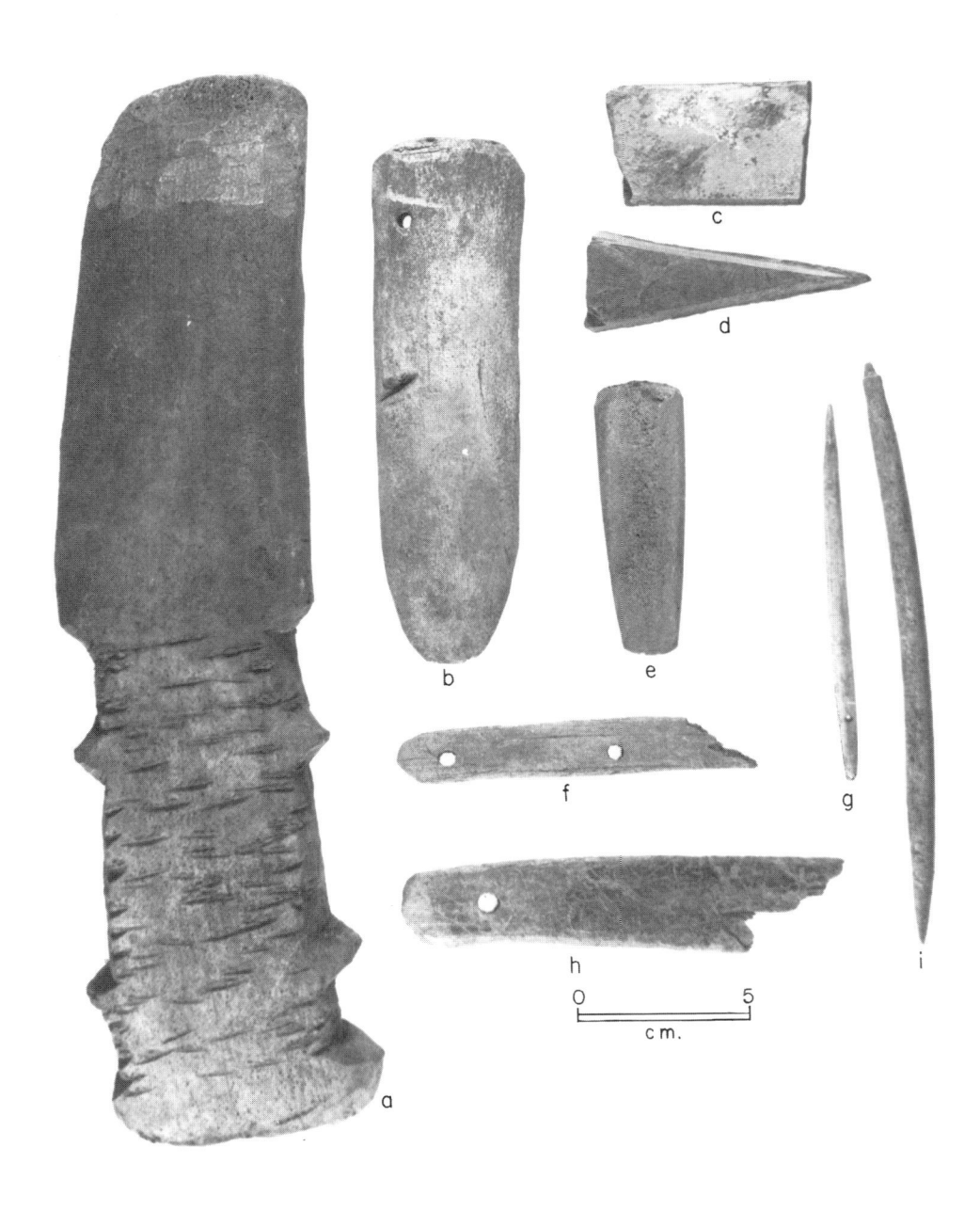

PLATE 18: IGLULUALUIT MEN'S TOOLS AND TRANSPORTATION ITEMS

165

PLATE 19: LANGTON BAY MEN'S TOOLS

FIGURE	DESCRIPTION AND CATALOGUE NUMBER	PAGE REFERENCE
a	e. and s.-blade knife handle: 60.1-3398	73
b	sideblade knife handle: 60.1-3215	74
c	endblade knife handle: 60.1-3296	73
d	endblade knife handle: 60.1-3298	73
e	endblade knife handle: 60.1-3304	73
f	endblade knife handle: 60.1-3399	73
g	endblade knife handle: 60.1-3400	73
h	endblade knife handle: 60.1-3319	73
i	endblade knife handle: 60.1-3401	73
j	endblade knife handle: 60.1-3299	73

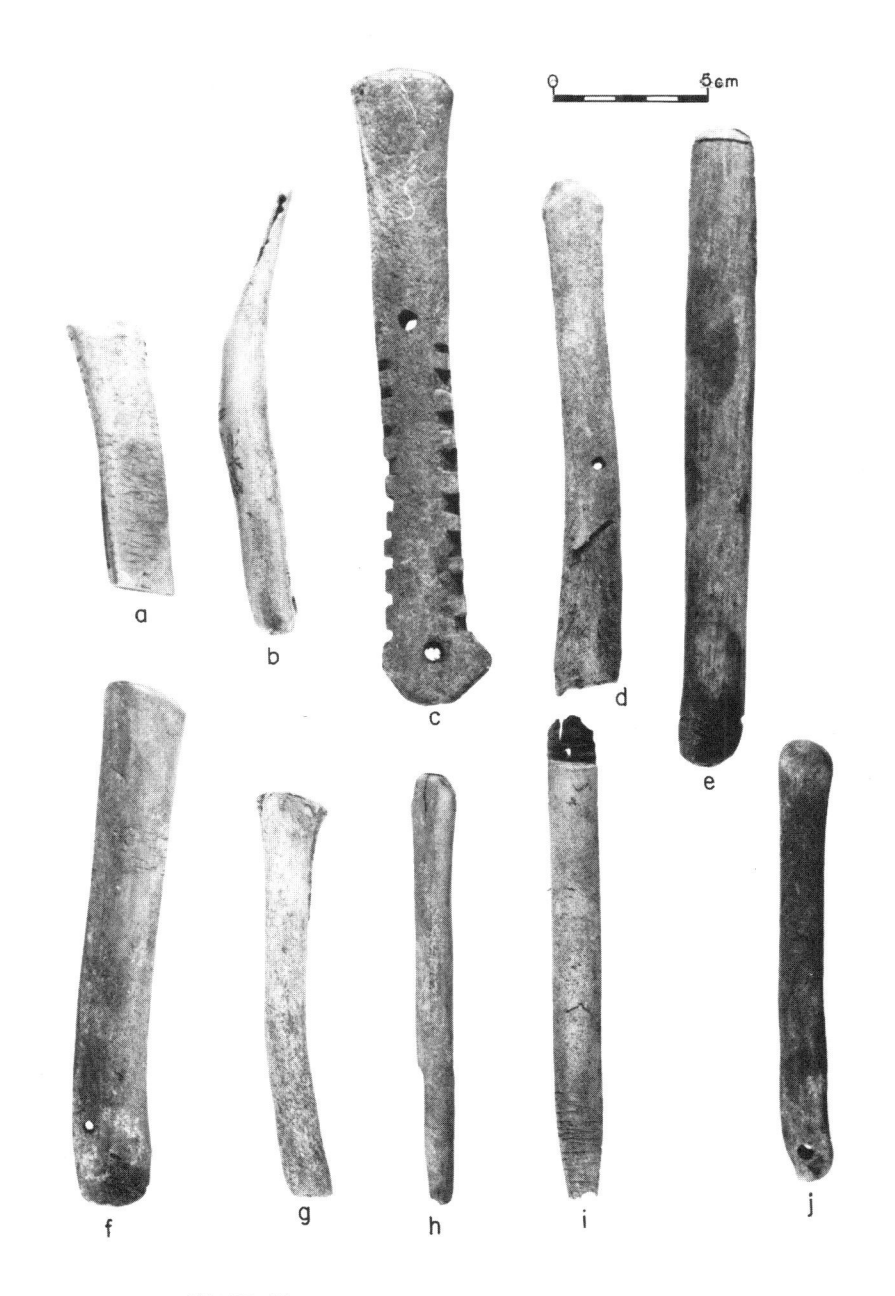

PLATE 19: LANGTON BAY MEN'S TOOLS

PLATE 20: LANGTON BAY MEN'S TOOLS AND TRANSPORTATION ITEMS

FIGURE	DESCRIPTION AND CATALOGUE NUMBER	PAGE REFERENCE
a	snow knife: 60.1-3294	74
b	wedge: 60.1-3402	74
c	wedge: 60.1-2962	74
d	sled shoe fragment: 60.1-3405	66
e	drill socket: 60.1-3319	74
f	drill socket: 60.1-3319	74
g	snow probe section: 60.1-3319	66

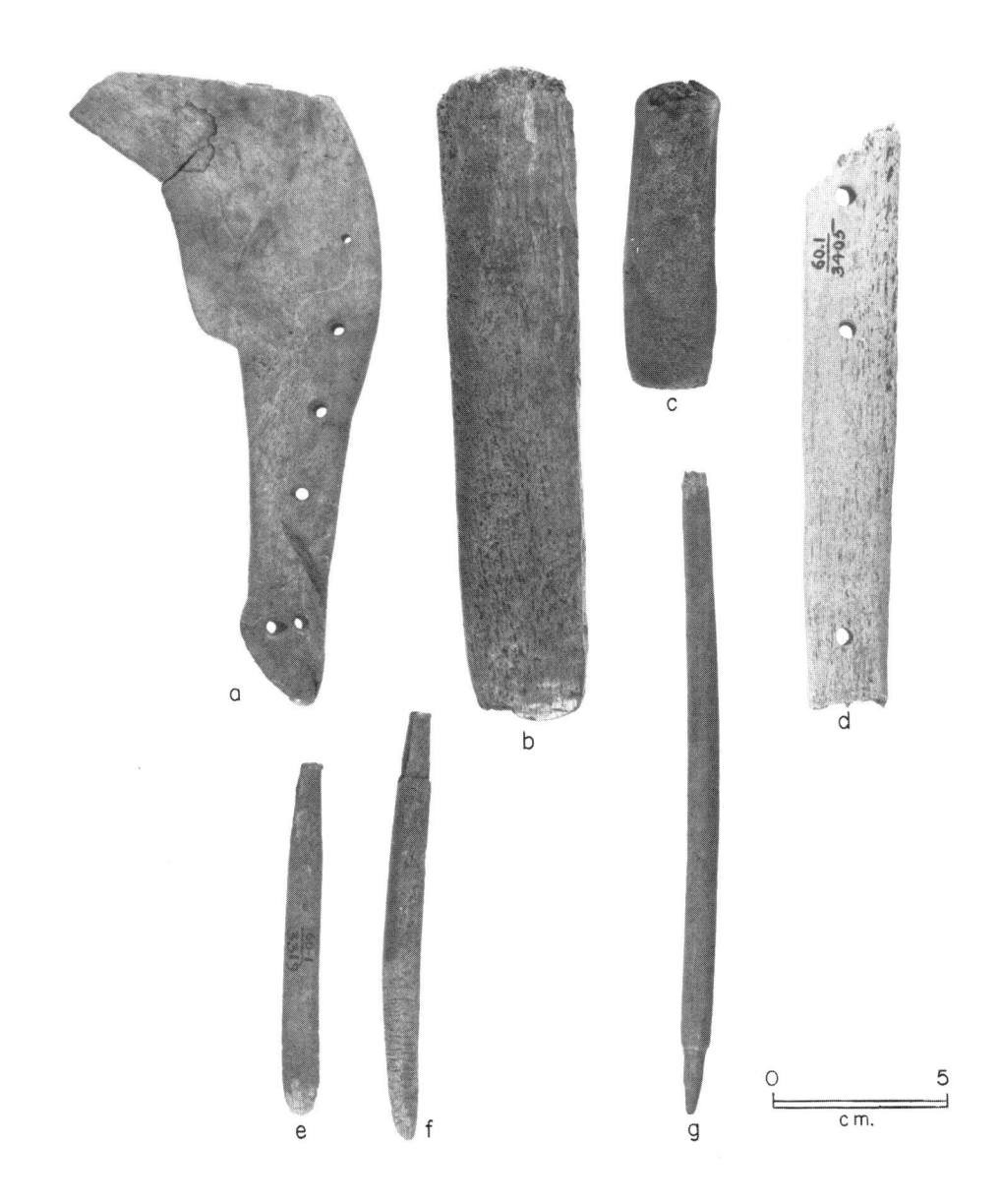

PLATE 20: LANGTON BAY MEN'S TOOLS AND TRANSPORTATION ITEMS

PLATE 21: OKAT MEN'S TOOLS

FIGURE	DESCRIPTION AND CATALOGUE NUMBER	PAGE REFERENCE
a	endblade knife handle: 60.1-3362	74
b	endblade knife handle: 60.1-2932	74
c	endblade knife handle: 60.1-3364	74
d	endblade knife handle: 60.1-2931	74
e	endblade knife handle: 60.1-3101	74
f	endblade knife handle: 60.1-2976	74
g	endblade knife handle: 60.1-2992	74
h	endblade knife handle: 60.1-3003	74
i	endblade knife handle: 60.1-2988	74
j	endblade knife handle: IX.D-86	74
k	sideblade knife handle: 60.1-2937	75

PLATE 21: OKAT MEN'S TOOLS

PLATE 22: OKAT MEN'S TOOLS

FIGURE	DESCRIPTION AND CATALOGUE NUMBER	PAGE REFERENCE
a	mattock: IX.D-68	76
b	adze head: 60.1-2943	75
c	adze head: IX.D-84	75
d	adze head: 60.1-2942	75
e	adze head: 60.1-2941	75

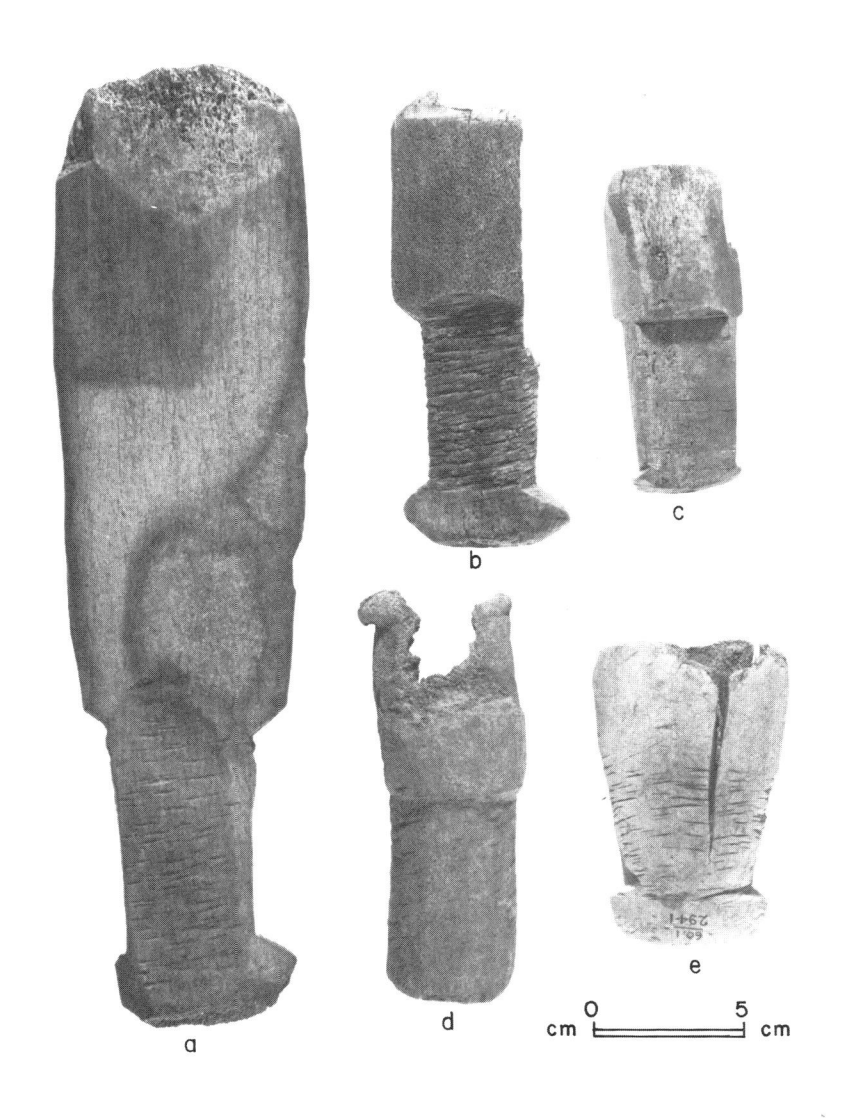

PLATE 22: OKAT MEN'S TOOLS

PLATE 23: OKAT MEN'S TOOLS AND TRANSPORTATION ITEMS

FIGURE	DESCRIPTION AND CATALOGUE NUMBER	PAGE REFERENCE
a	snow probe fragment: 60.1-2980	67
b	bone hammer: 60.1-3373	76
c	snow knife: 60.1-2940	76
d	sled shoe fragment: 60.1-2968	67
e	swivel pin: 60.1-3018	67
f	drill bit: IX.D-19	76

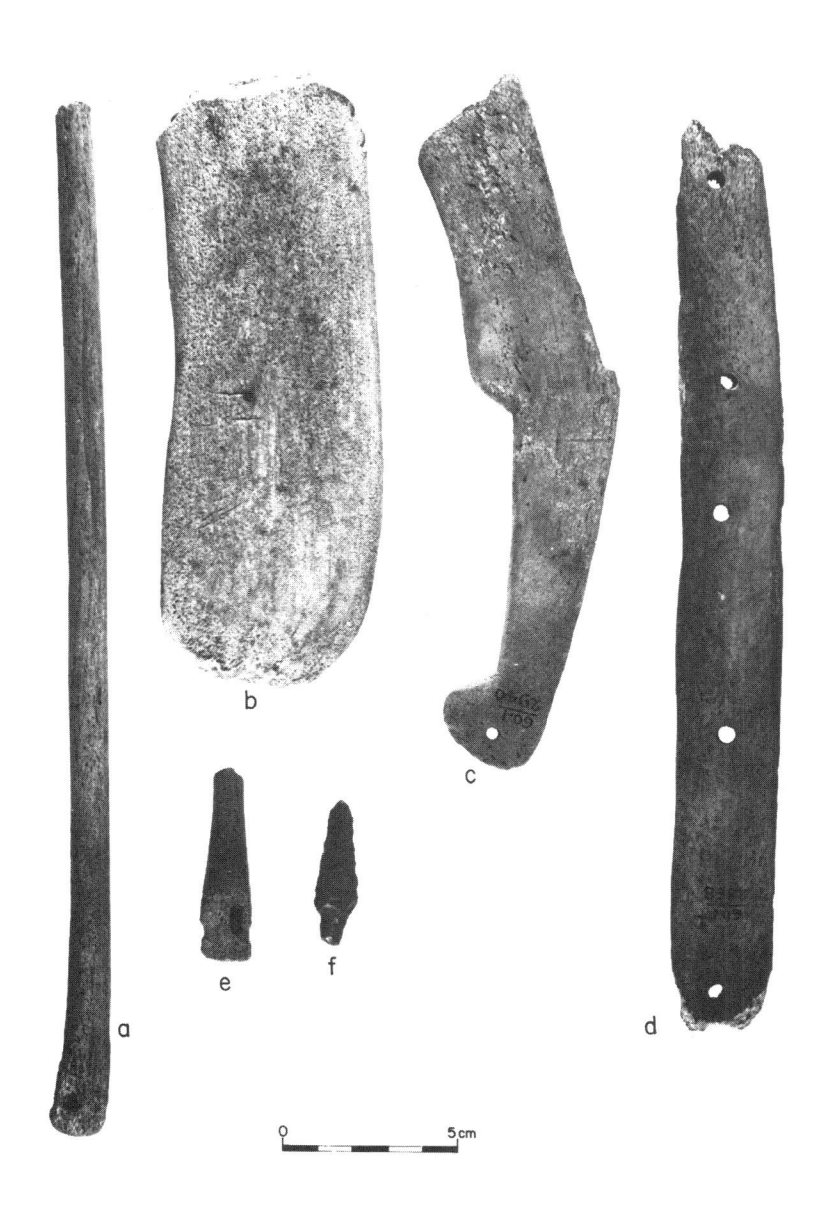

PLATE 23: OKAT MEN'S TOOLS AND TRANSPORTATION ITEMS

175

PLATE 24: BOOTH ISLAND MEN'S TOOLS

FIGURE	DESCRIPTION AND CATALOGUE NUMBER	PAGE REFERENCE
a	drill socket: IX.D-357	78
b	endblade knife handle: IX.D-278	77
c	endblade knife handle: IX.D-270	77
d	endblade knife handle: IX.D-277	77
e	sideblade knife handle: IX.D-272	77
f	drill socket: IX.D-358	78
g	sideblade knife handle: IX.D-271	77
h	composite knife handle: IX.D-365	77
i	graver handle: IX.D-280	77
j	graver with iron bit: IX.D-275	77

PLATE 24: BOOTH ISLAND MEN'S TOOLS

PLATE 25: BOOTH ISLAND MEN'S TOOLS

FIGURE	DESCRIPTION AND CATALOGUE NUMBER	PAGE REFERENCE
a	knife endblade blank: IX.D-288	77
b	slate knife endblade: IX.D-287b	77
c	slate knife endblade: IX.D-296ff	77
d	slate knife endblade: IX.D-287o	77
e	slate knife endblade: IX.D-287d	77
f	slate knife endblade: IX.D-287j	77
g	slate knife endblade: IX.D-285c	77
h	slate knife endblade: IX.D-285k	77
i	slate knife endblade: IX.D-285a	77
j	slate knife endblade: IX.D-285i	77
k	slate knife endblade: IX.D-287a	77
l	slate knife endblade: IX.D-287g	77
m	slate knife endblade: IX.D-285f	77

PLATE 25: BOOTH ISLAND MEN'S TOOLS

PLATE 26: BOOTH ISLAND MEN'S TOOLS

FIGURE	DESCRIPTION AND CATALOGUE NUMBER	PAGE REFERENCE
a	adze handle: IX.D-333	78
b	adze head: IX.D-311	78
c	wedge: IX.D-245	79
d	snow knife: IX.D-345	79
e	bone hammer: IX.D-323	79

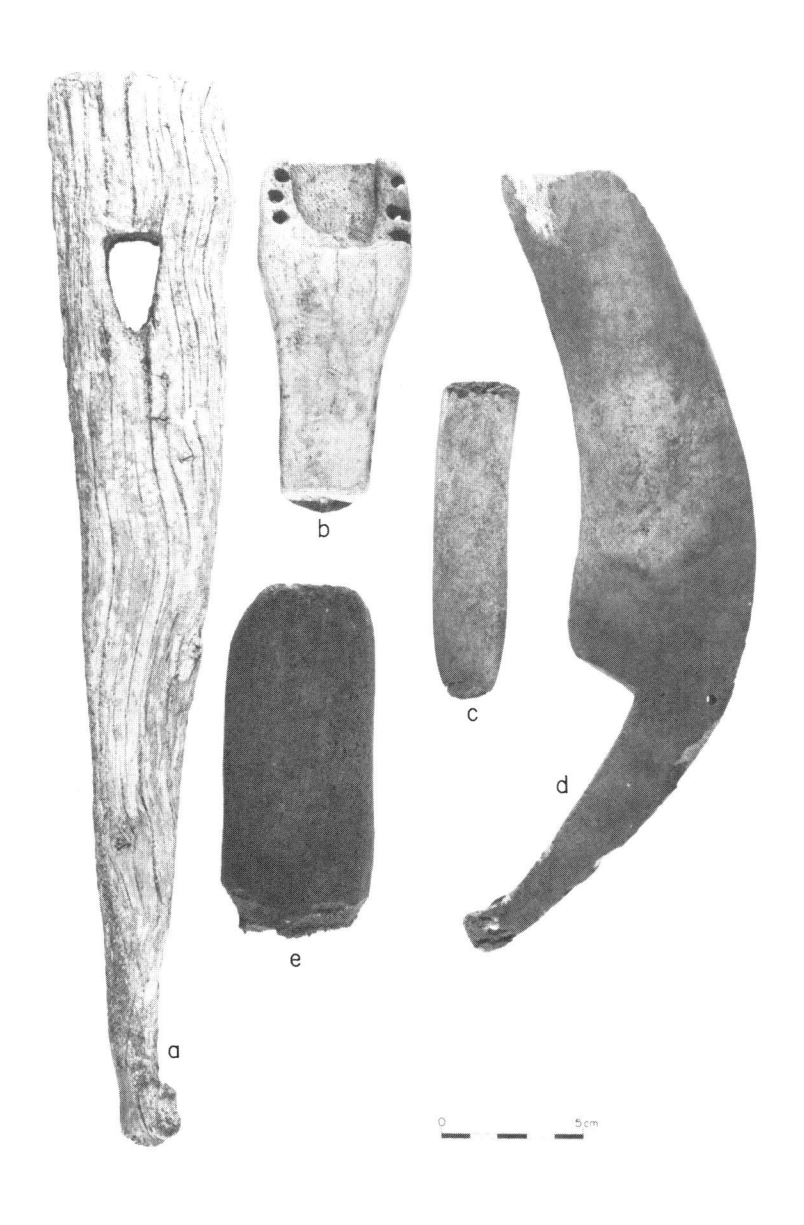

PLATE 26: BOOTH ISLAND MEN'S TOOLS

181

PLATE 27: BOOTH ISLAND MEN'S TOOLS AND TRANSPORTATION ITEMS

FIGURE	DESCRIPTION AND CATALOGUE NUMBER	PAGE REFERENCE
a	snow knife: IX.D-349	79
b	snow knife: IX.D-348	79
c	snow probe tip: IX.D-281dd	67
d	snow probe tip: IX.D-281x	67
e	snow probe handle: IX.D-306	67
f	sled shoe fragment: IX.D-239	67
g	sled shoe fragment: IX.D-237	67
h	snow probe tip: IX.D-281d	67
i	snow probe tip: IX.D-281o	67

PLATE 27: BOOTH ISLAND MEN'S TOOLS AND TRANSPORTATION ITEMS

183

PLATE 28: IGLULUALUIT WOMEN'S TOOLS AND ORNAMENTS

FIGURE	DESCRIPTION AND CATALOGUE NUMBER	PAGE REFERENCE
a	slate ulu blade: NlRu-1-366	85
b	slate ulu blade: NlRu-1-241	85
c	slate ulu blade: NlRu-1-230	85
d	antler spoon: NlRu-1-195	86
e	"fish scaler": NlRu-1-514	86
f	marrow spatula: NlRu-1-437	86
g	toy harpoon head: NlRu-1-448	87
h	endscraper: NlRu-1-372	85
i	endscraper: NlRu-1-402	85
j	endscraper: NlRu-1-330	85
k	endscraper: NlRu-1-139	85
l	endscraper: NlRu-1-193	85
m	endscraper: NlRu-1-335	85
n	pendant: NlRu-1-486	87
o	pendant: NlRu-1-519	87
p	pendant: NlRu-1-259	87
q	pendant: NlRu-1-107	87
r	button or clothing toggle: NlRu-1-58	87

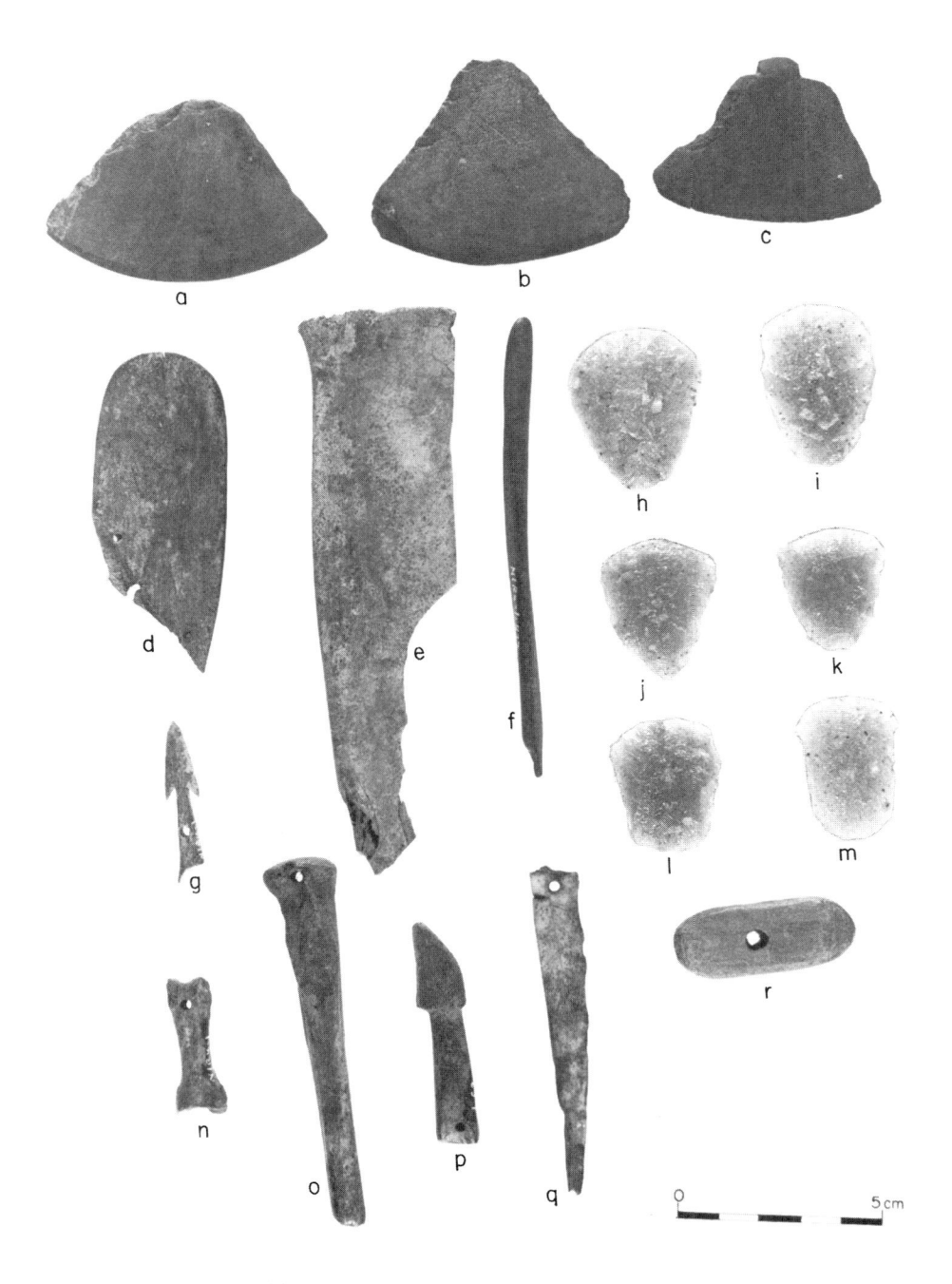

PLATE 28: IGLULUALUIT WOMEN'S TOOLS AND ORNAMENTS

185

PLATE 29: LANGTON BAY WOMEN'S TOOLS AND ORNAMENTS

FIGURE	DESCRIPTION AND CATALOGUE NUMBER	PAGE REFERENCE
a	ulu handle: 60.1-3300	88
b	ulu handle: 60.1-3006	88
c	scraper handle: 60.1-3396	88
d	scraper handle: 60.1-3397	88
e	scraper handle: 60.1-3297	88
f	bag handle: 60.1-3308	88
g	thimble holder: 60.1-3341	89
h	baleen shave: 60.1-3303	88
i	pendant: 60.1-3343	89
j	pendant: 60.1-3349	89
k	pendant: 60.1-3343	89
l	tubular bone bead: 60.1-3409	89

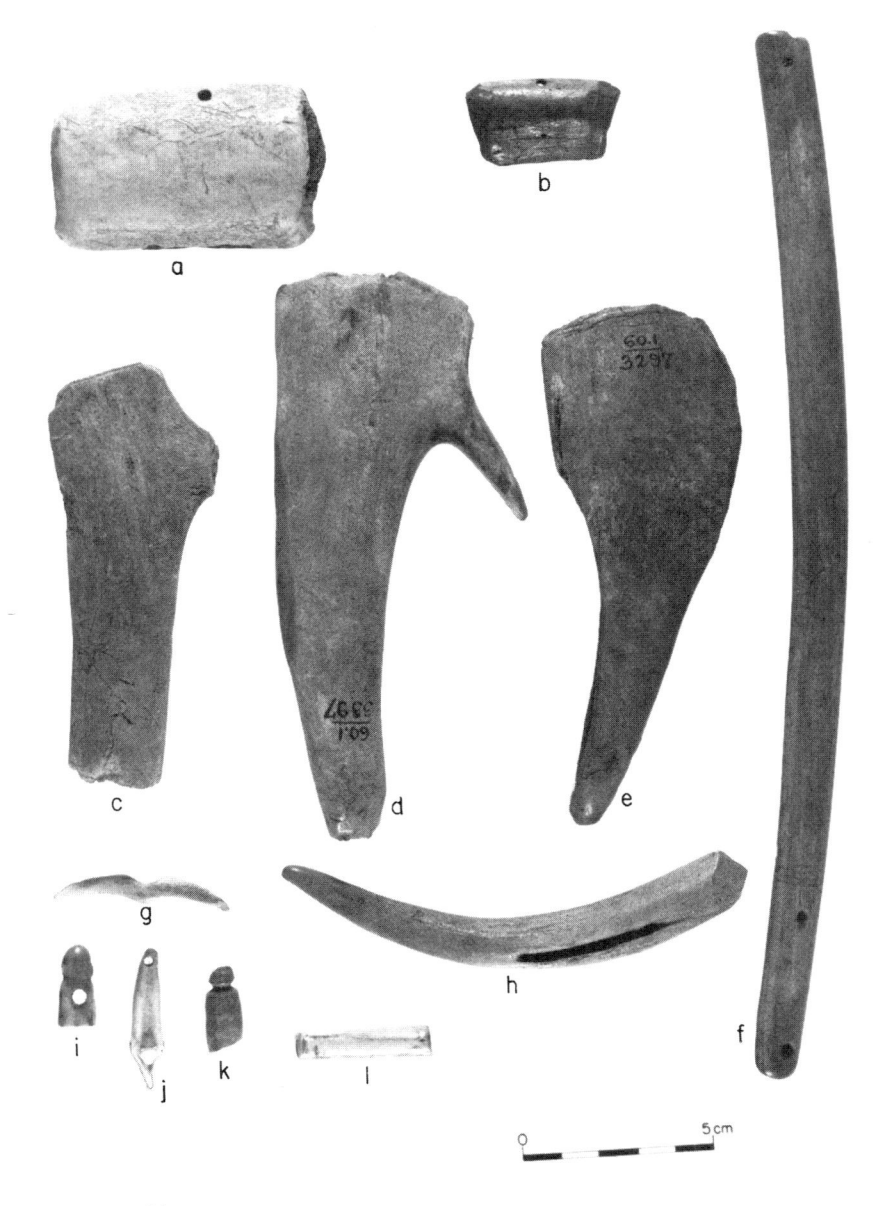

PLATE 29: LANGTON BAY WOMEN'S TOOLS AND ORNAMENTS

PLATE 30: OKAT WOMEN'S TOOLS

FIGURE	DESCRIPTION AND CATALOGUE NUMBER	PAGE REFERENCE
a	ulu handle: 60.1-2965	90
b	ulu handle: 60.1-2935	90
c	ulu handle: IX.D-71	90
d	ulu handle: 60.1-2934	90
e	ulu handle: 60.1-2936	90
f	ulu handle: IX.D-70	90
g	scraper handle: 60.1-2939	89
h	scraper handle: 60.1-2930	89
i	scraper handle: 60.1-2938	89
j	scraper handle: 60.1-2929	89
k	endscraper: IX.D-11j	89
l	endscraper: IX.D-11i	89
m	ulu blade fragment: IX.D-8a	90

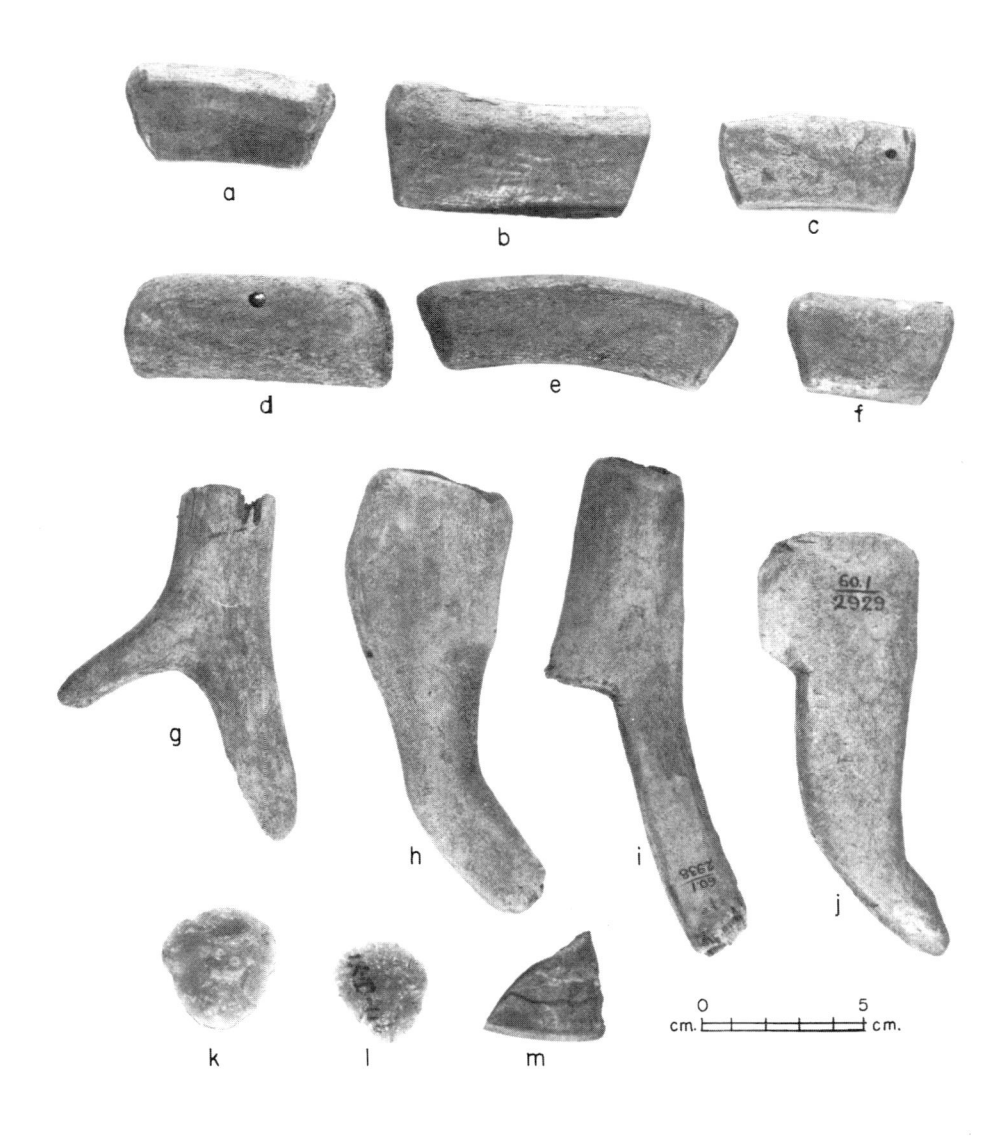

PLATE 30: OKAT WOMEN'S TOOLS

PLATE 31: OKAT WOMEN'S TOOLS

FIGURE	DESCRIPTION AND CATALOGUE NUMBER	PAGE REFERENCE
a	bag handle: 60.1-2972	89
b	scraper handle: IX.D-88	89
c	scraper handle: 60.1-2993	89
d	scraper handle: 60.1-3363	89
e	ulu handle: 60.1-3005	90
f	marrow spatula: 60.1-3030	90
g	ladle: 60.1-3357	90
h	antler knife: 60.1-3357	90

PLATE 31: OKAT WOMEN'S TOOLS

PLATE 32: BOOTH ISLAND WOMEN'S TOOLS

FIGURE	DESCRIPTION AND CATALOGUE NUMBER	PAGE REFERENCE
a	bone beamer: IX.D-216	91
b	ulu handle: IX.D-291	91
c	ulu handle: IX.D-292	91
d	ulu handle: IX.D-293	91
e	ulu blade: IX.D-293	93
f	ulu handle: IX.D-290	91
g	ulu blade: IX.D-289	93
h	ulu blade: IX.D-294b	93
i	ulu blade: IX.D-294f	93

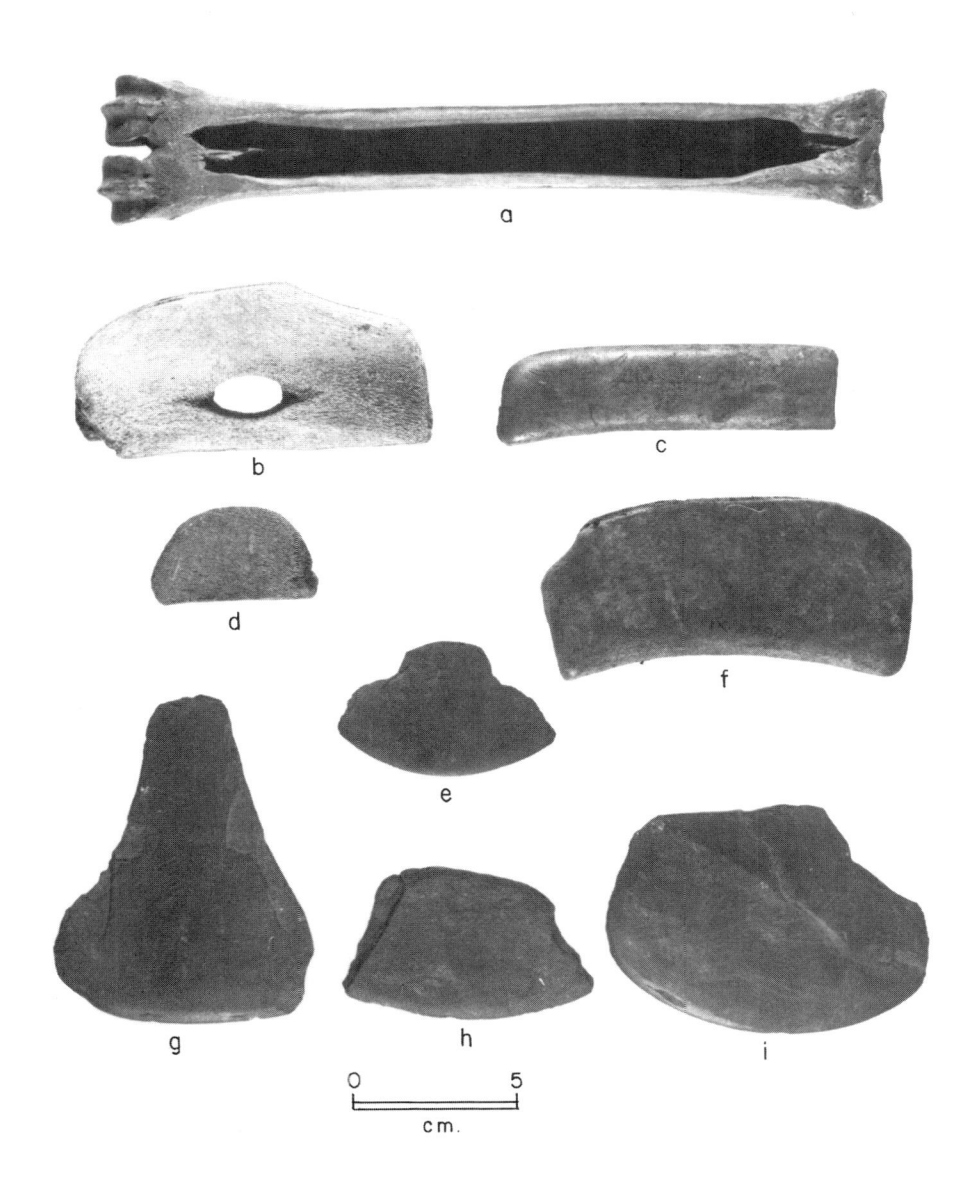

PLATE 32: BOOTH ISLAND WOMEN'S TOOLS

193

PLATE 33: BOOTH ISLAND WOMEN'S TOOLS AND ORNAMENTS

FIGURE	DESCRIPTION AND CATALOGUE NUMBER	PAGE REFERENCE
a	bag handle: IX.D-273	91
b	toy harpoon head: IX.D-274	93
c	pendant: IX.D-317	93
d	bone bead: IX.D-320	93
e	antler comb: IX.D-322	94
f	bone tube: IX.D-248	-
g	endscraper: IX.D-284d	91
h	endscraper: IX.D-284c	91
i	endscraper fragment: IX.D-284a	91
j	endscraper: IX.D-284b	91
k	uniface: IX.D-283	-
l	pottery vessel rim: IX.D-213	91

PLATE 33: BOOTH ISLAND WOMEN'S TOOLS AND ORNAMENTS

195

PLATE 34: IGLULUALUIT POTTERY

FIGURE	DESCRIPTION AND CATALOGUE NUMBER	PAGE REFERENCE
a	Class 1 rim sherd: NlRu-1-39	83
b	Class 2 rim sherd: NlRu-1-43	83
c	Class 2 rim sherd: NlRu-1-206	83
d	Class 1 rim sherd: NlRu-1-85	83
e	Class 3 rim sherd: NlRu-1-115	83
f	Class 4 base sherd: NlRu-1-40	83
g	Class 4 base sherd: NlRu-1-203	83

PLATE 34: IGLULUALUIT POTTERY

PLATE 35: IGLULUALUIT POTTERY

FIGURE	DESCRIPTION AND CATALOGUE NUMBER	PAGE REFERENCE
upper	Class 4 pottery vessel, rim and base: NlRu-1-264	83
lower	Class 1 pottery vessel: NlRu-1-36	83

PLATE 35: IGLULUALUIT POTTERY

PLATE 36: IGLULUALUIT MISCELLANEOUS WOODEN ARTIFACTS

FIGURE	DESCRIPTION AND CATALOGUE NUMBER	PAGE REFERENCE
a	whale effigy: NlRu-1-391	87
b	ulu handle: NlRu-1-466	85
c	handle: NlRu-1-282	84
d	fish spear prong: NlRu-1-272	57
e	drill spindle: NlRu-1-125	72
f	drill spindle: NlRu-1-446	72

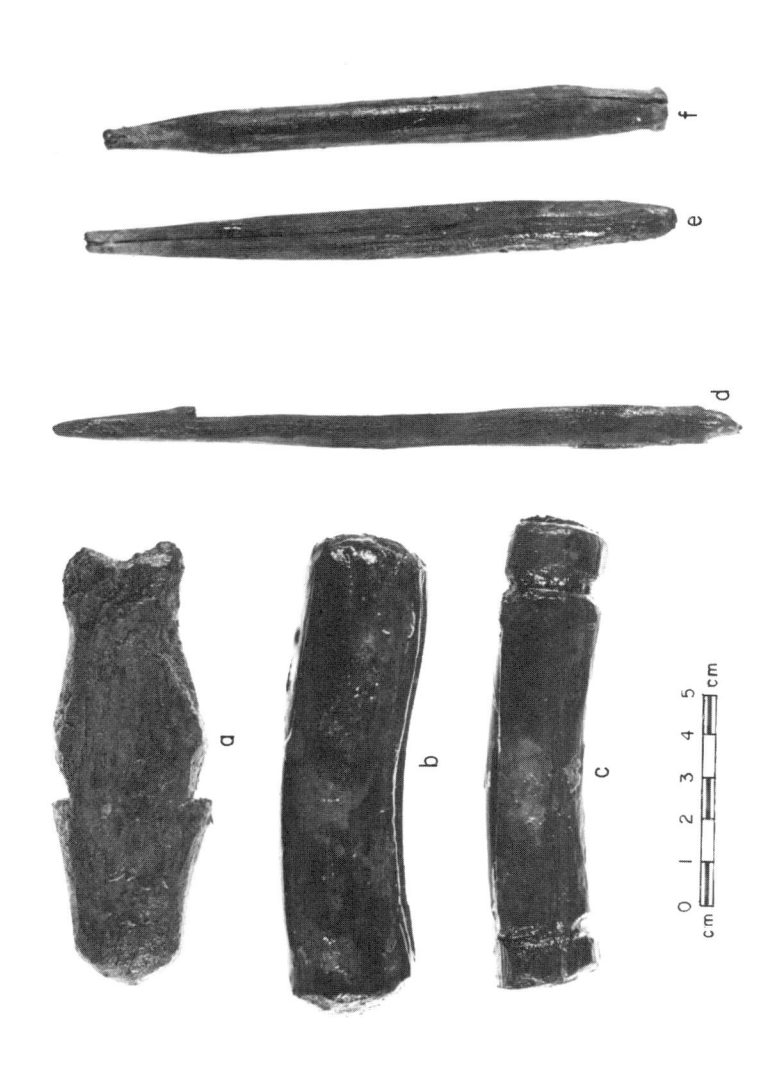

PLATE 36: IGLULUALUIT MISCELLANEOUS WOODEN ARTIFACTS